LITERATURE AND LANGUAGE DIVISION
THE CHICAGO PUBLIC LIBRARY
400 SOUTH STATE STREET
CHICAGO, ILLINOIS 60605

A Map of Doubt and Rescue

Ꮖ

A PLAY BY

Susan Miller

 University of Tampa Press • Tampa, Florida • 2004

Copyright © 2004 by Susan Miller. All rights reserved.

On the dust jacket: Charlotte Salomon, "Life? or Theatre?" gouache, 1940-42
Collection of Jewish Historical Museum, Amsterdam
Copyright © Charlotte Salomon Foundation

Manufactured in the United States of America
Book design by Richard Mathews
Printed on acid-free paper ∞
First Edition

No part of this book may be reproduced, stored in a retrieval system, or transmitted in any form or by any means, electronic, mechanical, photocopying, recording, or otherwise, except as may be expressly permitted by the applicable copyright statutes or in writing by the publisher. All inquiries concerning performance rights to the play should be addressed to The Joyce Ketay Agency, 630 Ninth Avenue, Suite 706, New York, N.Y. 10036. Visit Susan Miller online at www.susanmillerplaywright.com

University of Tampa Press
401 West Kennedy Blvd.
Tampa, FL 33606

ISBN 1-879852-28-4
ISBN 1-879852-29-2 (pbk.)

Browse & order online at
http://utpress.ut.edu

Library of Congress Cataloging-in-Publication Data

Miller, Susan, 1944-
A map of doubt and rescue : a play / by Susan Miller.
  p. cm.
ISBN 1-879852-28-4 (hardback : alk. paper) -- ISBN 1-879852-29-2 (pbk. : alk. paper)
I. Title.
PS3613.I554M55 2004
812'.6--dc22
                              2004018594

R03134 29703

For making so much possible –
I dedicate this play to my parents,
Thelma and Isaac Figlin,
my son, Jeremy,
and to Lida

Acknowledgments

I am grateful to The John Simon Guggenheim Memorial Foundation for its support of my work. Leigh Silverman, who took a leap of faith at the beginning. Abigail Deser, for her passion, intelligence, and determination in helping me find the play. And the remarkable cast of Ojai, who brought me to tears with their talent and love.

A Map of Doubt And Rescue was developed in workshop by New York Stage and Film and The Ojai Playwrights Conference. It is the winner of the Susan Smith Blackburn Prize for the Best Play by a Woman in the English language and the 2004 Pinter Review Prize for Drama.

Cast, director, and playwright at the Ojai Playwrights Conference Workshop, August 2004. Photo by Bruce Botnick.

Production History

Ojai Playwrights Conference – Workshop. August 2004.
Artistic Director, Robert H. Egan. Directed by Abigail Deser.

The cast was as follows.

Hannah/ Josie/ Maggie • *Judith Light*
Editor • *Michael Gross*
Homer/ Dad/ Mr. Frank/ Seymour • *Paul Adelstein*
Young Josie/ Anne Frank/ Actress1/ Gir • *Liza Weil*
Woman in Cafe/ Mom/ Actress2/ Winnie • *Nealla Gordon*
Delany/ Interviewer/ Volunteer • *Leo Marks*
Man 2/ Meyer/ Firefighter/ Sugarman • *Zachary Quinto*
Claire/ Actress3/ Rachel/ Tour Guide • *Karen Aldridge*

ભ

New York Stage and Film at Vassar – Workshop. July 2000.
Producing directors: Mark Linn-Baker, Max Mayer, Leslie Urdang.
Managing Producer, Johanna Pfaelzer. Directed by Judy Minor

The cast was as follows:

Hannah/Josie/Maggie • *Leslie Lyles*
Editor • *Robert Hogan*
Homer/Dad/Mr.Frank/Seymour • *Frank Wood*
Young Josie/ Anne Frank/ Actress1/Girl • *Angela Goethals*
Woman in Cafe/Mom/ Actress1/Winnie • *Welker White*
Delaney/ Interviewer/Volunteer • *Anthony Arkin*
Man 2/ Meyer/ Firefighter/ Sugarman • *Justin Hagin*
Claire/ Actress3/ Rachel/ Tour Guide • *Michelle Powers*

The Characters

HANNAH / JOSIE / MAGGIE
(in her forties or fifties)

WOMAN IN CAFE / MOM / ACTRESS 2 / WINNIE / POET / PLAYWRIGHT'S WIFE
(in her thirties or forties)

CLAIRE / ACTRESS 3 / RACHEL / TOUR GUIDE
(in her twenties)

YOUNG JOSIE / ANNE FRANK / ACTRESS 1 / GIRL / ANYA DIVAC
(in her late teens to early twenties)

EDITOR
(in his fifties)

HOMER / DAD / MR. FRANK / SEYMOUR / DONALD
(in his thirties or forties)

DELANEY / INTERVIEWER / MAN 1 / VOLUNTEER / BOBBY
(in his thirties)

MAN 2 / MEYER / FIREMAN / SUGARMAN
(in his twenties)

Act One

ACT ONE

Everyone Makes Mistakes

The faint, old-fashioned sound of a typewriter, though this is present time. As lights up on a small newspaper office, Ben Holiday, the EDITOR, *sits on the edge of his desk, reading a page of newspaper copy. He runs a pencil through it in between fast swallows of coffee.* DELANEY, *one of the staff writers, walks in.*

DELANEY: I hope that's not my piece you're taking the pencil to.

EDITOR: It's mine.

DELANEY: You had a chance yet to —

EDITOR: *(Looking at pages.)* I like it. The one about — the woman. Where she sends the card. The one about the woman who sends the same card.

DELANEY: Two years in a row.

EDITOR: At least she sends a card.

DELANEY: She's distraught.

EDITOR: I like this. I like how you put it.

DELANEY: She doesn't want the person who gets the same card two years in a row to think he doesn't matter.

EDITOR: Of course not. Of course she doesn't. You're tender with the facts. That's nice, Delaney. We'll use it. Question, though.

DELANEY: Yeah?

EDITOR: On the other piece. Clear this up for me. You say the Steins invite the single guy over for dinner. He's new. You cover that. He's new to the — whatever.

DELANEY: University. Teaches constitutional law.

EDITOR: He's single. He's new. All right. What's his name —

DELANEY: Morgan.

EDITOR: Morgan shows up. Steins aren't home. Now, they forget what night? Or this is so unimportant to them they don't remember extending?

DELANEY: The invitation. You're saying — of course. You're saying — I mean, it makes all the difference.

EDITOR: Because what are you conveying here? They forget the night, which is one thing, or they forget him. They forget the man. Which is — well. What exactly is the lapse?

DELANEY: Because if — right.

EDITOR: See.

DELANEY: Because this changes the level. If they forgot the man.

EDITOR: But, if it's the night they got wrong —

DELANEY: They feel bad. The Steins. They feel terrible.

EDITOR: I know. But, just what exactly is the lapse.

DELANEY: I'll see what I can glean.

(Starts to leave)

EDITOR: Lovely take on the greeting card situation.

(DELANEY is gone. EDITOR turns towards the audience as he begins to speak directly to them. He is invigorated, troubled, and wholly in love with his work.)

EDITOR: I write the Mistake Column for the *Sun Times*. Here in Hudson. People write in and say — this happened or that. Small errors. Touching faux pas. Achingly minor wrongs. You'd be surprised, or maybe not, how many people want to place an incident with me. Everyone makes mistakes.

(Beat.)

It came to me that we already have things in place to catalogue our deaths, our vows, our crimes. I just happen to think there are still things left to name.

(He picks up a piece of paper.)

Sometimes I'll come upon a letter with such steep shame. "Dear Mistake Finder, I've turned my husband's undershirts and shorts all to pink. Everyone knows not to combine the colors with the whites. Everyone knows that. I'm in disgrace."

(Beat.)

Well, no. Disgrace would be — if you were, say, a shrink and you let your emotions get carried away and crossed the line with your patient who was making progress in her life and caused her confusion and difficulty. Or you passed a smug cruelty to a person struggling just to make it out her door and back in one piece and you added to her misery.

(Beat.)

But as much as I'd like to make it easier on the person who screwed up the laundry and tell her she's done no real harm, her troubles are her troubles. And it's a holy list, a holy accounting — what's given to me — what people place in my hands.

(Beat.)

Before this, I had the Lost and Found column. Well, my version of it. By lost and found I don't mean objects. I don't mean keys or wallets or even precious animals. A person can lose heart. A person can lose his footing.

(Beat.)

EDITOR: You go along and you're sure of some things. The way it feels to say hello to the guy who sells you coffee in the morning. Or walking up the porch steps, the feel of the varnish on the railing wood. How the touch of that secures you to a place. A person can lose his touch. His vitality. His voice. His true voice. But, by the same sudden way that it left, a thing can return. Found: Manny's sense of humor, restored to him by one sweet and fetching Eleanor Smigel. Who laughed at the right moment.

(Beat.)

Anyhow, one afternoon, about a month into the column, I was at my desk, and a man, somehow not unfamiliar to me, walked into my office and came to be my turning point. He seemed startled. Actually *startled* by the appearance of everything in the normal world. It's like you wanted to lead him by the hand, point to things, say: Door. Desk. Man.

(HOMER *enters and the scene is re-created.*)

EDITOR: Yes?

HOMER: Can I — come in?

EDITOR: You want to come in.

HOMER: I was — I was —

EDITOR: Yes.

HOMER: I was placing an ad. I was down the hall.

EDITOR: Down the hall? You were placing an ad down the hall?

HOMER: I wanted to sell something. And now I'm questioning whether —

EDITOR: Now you don't want to.

HOMER: It's that how can you — how can you — I was placing an ad, writing it up. I mean someone was writing it up. And she asked me to describe the item. The item she called it. The item you want to sell. And I just — do you mind if I — I might have to sit down.

EDITOR: You were saying, though.

HOMER: I'm not sure. I'm not sure now.

EDITOR: About selling.

HOMER: I'm not myself.

EDITOR: It happens.

HOMER: No, but, really.

EDITOR: Not what you used to be.

HOMER: That. And —

EDITOR: And?

HOMER: And — not what — I — am. Not — excuse me.

EDITOR: What were you selling?

HOMER: Excuse me for this.

EDITOR: What was the thing you were selling?

HOMER: Just something that belonged to me. I thought I was finished with it.

EDITOR: Well, you don't have to. Sell it. You can turn around and go right home. You don't have to sell anything.

HOMER: I lost my reason.

EDITOR: *(Shaken.)* That's — yes. That's —

HOMER: It was just something I had that belonged to me.

(Beat.)

You'd think — you'd think —

EDITOR: Did someone send you to see me or —

HOMER: You'd think, though — just a thing like that.

EDITOR: Well. It's fragile. It's a fragile hold we've got.

HOMER: I'm not always like this.

EDITOR: No. I know. I —

(Beat.)

You look so familiar. Like somebody I went through something with.

HOMER: I don't think so. But it could have been.

EDITOR: Maybe just someone I admired in school.

HOMER: *(After a moment.)* I'm not myself.

(HOMER leaves.)

EDITOR: *(To audience)* And that's the day I got out of Lost and Found. Mistakes don't come wandering in the door. I'm more at ease with mistakes.

(Beat.)

Here's something we ran last week.

(Reads.)

"I'm a gardener. I pride myself on the details. On knowing the species and seasons of most non human living things. I measure most things by the way a seed takes its time, takes hold. You can scoff, but I am pleased to haul tons of dirt. And when there's a bloom — lilac, or geranium, I'm gratified. Tomatoes. Oh, I could go on about them. And I want to tell you that weeds, though I'm constrained to remove them, I am not their willing executioner. Weeds, in case you didn't know, have their own variety. The Pearly Everlasting. Sweet Everlasting. I'm a lucky man to work in pastures and hillsides and backyards. My clients trust me to make good on what's available to them in the way of a better life. So, I take my work seriously. That's why it's so hard to tell you this. But, if I don't you'll come upon it someday and — all right, the short of it is, I mixed up the Anderson's tulips with the Henderson's. Different soil. They'll both perish."

(Beat.)

Some people can live with their mistakes. The rest of us are tortured by them.

(Beat.)

There are days I would just like to wear a disguise when I go out. Like the restaurant critics. But I'm sure people would catch on to me. Or I'd give myself away. It just seems natural for people to tell me things. Like this one afternoon.

(Beat.)

I was over at the Cafe.

(He turns his desk around to be a table, as a WOMAN *walks into the area carrying a small table. She pulls up a chair behind it and sits.)*

WOMAN: I had it written down. The time and date. I had it written in my calendar. I had it written all the way across the page. Twelve noon. Now how do you get mixed up about twelve noon? I was supposed to meet him at the cafe near the train station. That's when he was getting in. Well, 11:50. I was eager. Things can work out. Some things work out. Don't they?

EDITOR: *(To audience.)* I was having my coffee. I was distracted by her. By the presence of someone so — disappointed.

WOMAN: He didn't come. I was late. He didn't come.

EDITOR: He might have. He might have come and left.

WOMAN: I missed him. I was late, and he thought I wasn't coming. And he left. I had been here already. I had been to the cafe hours before. I was so early, I took a walk. I didn't want to be seen as eager. So I took a walk. And I imagined our meeting. I walked and conjured our meeting. I saw him move toward me. I was drawn to him. I saw a future in it. I walked and the future was in my thoughts. And I went too far past the time of our meeting.

(Beat.)

You think — you hope — something's finally going to work out.

EDITOR: It can still.

WOMAN: No.

EDITOR: You can go and look for him.

WOMAN: No.

EDITOR: Find him and tell him.

WOMAN: He left. He took the next train. He went.

EDITOR: She was ragged. Her hair fell on to her forehead. Maybe he wasn't on a train. Maybe he took a room for the night. Maybe he'd go back the next day and look for her.

WOMAN: I never should've —

EDITOR: She was disconsolate.

WOMAN: I never should've —

(EDITOR *turns to audience.*)

EDITOR: It had all the right ingredients.

(Beat.)

I ran it.

(The WOMAN *leaves, followed immediately by the entrance of* DEL- ANEY *and another young staff writer,* CLAIRE TURNER.*)*

EDITOR: Okay, what've you got? Turner, give us this day.

CLAIRE: *(Looking at her notes.)* A friend of Jane Lowell's asks her how her husband is. Jane bursts into tears. Friend forgot he moved out. Left Jane for someone else.

EDITOR: Uh huh. Nice. Nice.

DELANEY: I got something over at the high school. Librarian stamped the wrong date. Gave a sophomore three years to return *Franny And Zooey.*

EDITOR: Sources?

DELANEY: I got a look at the book. Librarian's a — have you seen her? Librarian's an M.F.A. out of Smith or somewhere. Legs up to here. You haven't seen her? Any excuse now, kids off to the stacks. She'll be fine.

CLAIRE: The Maxwell dinner party. Al Delmonico showed up in a tux.

EDITOR: I know. I happened to be there. He looked classy. Shiny. He shone.

CLAIRE: He's really embarrassed, though.

EDITOR: He was a thing of beauty. But, he was not feeling beautiful. So, I went home and put mine on to keep him company. Didn't miss much, anyhow. Those tired hors d'oeuvres.

(Beat.)

We got a picture?

(DELANEY *hands him a sheaf of glossy photos.)*

EDITOR: *(Commenting as he studies the photos.)* Al looking sheepish.

(Looking at another one.)

Al before they slap on the handcuffs, it looks like.

(The next one.)

Al sweet on Mrs. Al.

(Beat.)

I think Al sheepish is our man. If we go with Al, we go Al sheepish.

DELANEY: All right, how about this. Mike Neapolitan is thanking everyone in his retirement speech — thanks his colleagues, secretary of twenty-five years, thanks his old alma mater, kudos to the fellas who played poker every Wednesday, his gumbas. Thanks for the memories to his mother, may she rest in peace, hurrahs to the company and the sweet benefits package they retire him with. Gets his laughs and applause. All the smoky hail and fare wells. Goes home. Hell. He forgot to thank his wife. Never mentioned her name. Not a word about the woman who put up with him all these years.

(Beat.)

He's sick over it. She's icy. He's gotta tell.

(Beat.)

Bears considering.

CLAIRE: That's a lock. Don't you think?

EDITOR: *(After a moment.)* A person thinks another person loves him, when she doesn't. Takes her words wrong. As declarations. Takes her awkwardness as tender steps in his direction. He speaks too soon.

(Beat.)

Something like that. Give me something like that.

CLAIRE: Are you saying fabricate?

EDITOR: This exists. What I'm talking about. This is out there. This is in supply. There is no lack.

DELANEY: I've got a Sugarman, fellow out in Los Angeles, wants to apologize to his mother for going into the movie business.

EDITOR: He regrets this? He thinks, what, he should've —

DELANEY: I don't know. He wants to — he's sorry. Sorry for —

EDITOR: I'm worried with regard to apologies. That's something a person does himself in his own voice, one on one. It's a private matter.

CLAIRE: I thought you said —

EDITOR: I know — I said — one time I said — I know that. But, it's personal.

DELANEY: He has a belief this was the biggest mistake of his life.

EDITOR: *(Sincere.)* I'm sorry to hear that. I am sorry.

DELANEY: Which is when you think about it, just so — I mean, considering Sugarman, he's what — 24, 25 — and he just sold a screenplay. Or an idea for a screenplay. Well, anyhow, it was something to do with a movie. He just sold something to the movies, so you'd think he'd be —

EDITOR: That's just it. Why we can't run apologies is it's too early to tell. He's young. He doesn't know what it's going to be. It's too soon to know what a thing will turn out to be.

DELANEY: He's saying it wasn't honest.

EDITOR: What he wrote? What he wrote wasn't honest?

DELANEY: I think that's what he —

EDITOR: Or what he did? The things he had to do.

DELANEY: Look, the man says he made a mistake. He wants to apologize. To his mother!

EDITOR: Well, we should all apologize to our mothers. Can I see the letter?

(CLAIRE hands him the letter and he starts to read it to himself.)

EDITOR: Sugarman's got a way with a sentence. You get relief. That's what you get from a good sentence. You come to the end, you feel relieved.

(Lights up on a young man, SUGARMAN, in his own space, talking as he writes.)

SUGARMAN: It's the middle of the night. Waiting to begin. How many others are writing to you at this very instant. Do you love us? I'm a young man. And I'm already sorry for a number of things. You could say I'm constant, anyhow.

(Lights off SUGARMAN.)

EDITOR: *(Puts Sugarman's letter down.)* He's at a loss.

CLAIRE: What do we do?

EDITOR: So here's a strict moment. Do we go on with the column the way it is or break down a young man's disappointment in himself into an argument for change? Dissolve the properties of the word "mistake" and imbue it with some kind of glorious, shattering possibility. And in that, see why it is we punish ourselves and think if we don't choose right, we'll ruin everything.

CLAIRE: *(Bringing him back.)* You want to dip into the backlog?

(CLAIRE and DELANEY look through their folders and begin to rattle off a list of possibilities.)

CLAIRE: There's a mix-up on the ingredients in a famous chocolate cake recipe.

DELANEY: Mailman delivers a letter to the wrong address. Turns out the husband in one house is having an affair with the wife in the other. Adultery is exposed and mailman is depressed over the suffering.

CLAIRE: Thelma Page goes to introduce her new boyfriend, calls him by her ex's name.

EDITOR: *(To audience.)* I've had a couple of crazy offers. Syndication was one. Then a book deal. The best of the worst. A year's end review. Highlights from the past mistakes and can we learn from them type of affair. But some things are just what they are. They aren't meant to be made into anything more. That's how you ruin things. That would be a mistake.

DELANEY: Here's one I'm liking for today.

(He reads.)

"Dear Editor, I made the same mistake. I made the same mistake twice. I feel like a fool."

EDITOR: *(To audience.)* Maybe there's only one mistake you keep making. That's yours. Your mistake. Your whole life you try to correct, but it's in the cells. It's your map. It's what you're put here for. The one thing you own. The one and only thing that's for certain yours. You're here to make it and you're here to make up for it. You think you're pursuing a career. You're bringing up the children. You're educating yourself. But, you're just after a correction.

DELANEY: Ben?

EDITOR: I don't know.

DELANEY: What do we run? What's our week?

EDITOR: Let's give Al the Wednesday edition. Tag it with the guy doesn't thank his wife.

CLAIRE: And Friday?

DELANEY: We go out with Sugarman's apology to Mom? See what it brings.

EDITOR: *(Struggling with his decision.)* It's just not a mistake yet. It's too soon to know.

(CLAIRE and DELANEY start to leave.)

DELANEY: Keep my ears open for that loving the wrong person kind of occurrence. Some such like that.

(On the heels of their departure, just as BEN returns to his desk, his cold coffee and his decisions, Ben's wife, HANNAH, enters. He is surprised to see her.)

EDITOR: Hannah!

HANNAH: Everything's fine. Everything's fine.

EDITOR: I didn't expect you, that's all.

HANNAH: Nothing terrible happened. Everyone's fine.

EDITOR: Good. I'm glad to see you here. It's been so long since you've come down. You don't come down.

HANNAH: The afternoon was gaining on me. It was just — I needed to get out of the situation. The situation of being home.

(She touches his chair with familiarity.)

I brought you a clean shirt.

EDITOR: *(Touched.)* You did that?

HANNAH: I used to know all your shirts by heart.

EDITOR: So this is just an anonymous shirt?

HANNAH: Ben —

EDITOR: Why is it that a heart soars for no reason except maybe your wife brought you a shirt?

HANNAH: I made a terrible mistake.

EDITOR: Whatever it was — I'm sure whatever it was doesn't matter.

HANNAH: I want to — god, this is — but if I don't say it —

EDITOR: If you don't say it.

HANNAH: Listen, Ben. If I don't say it, then every day is false. Every day I don't say it is false, and you're so forgiving. Every thing you write is a statement of forgiveness. But, then why am I so scared ?

EDITOR: Hannah.

HANNAH: I have to get away for awhile.

EDITOR: I should've called you last night. I was working. It got to be so late. I didn't want to wake you.

HANNAH: I love waking to you. It's not waking to you that's hard.

EDITOR: I get distracted.

HANNAH: You don't even know.

EDITOR: What?

HANNAH: You haven't even noticed.

EDITOR: What?

HANNAH: My distraction.

(Beat.)

I'm going away, Ben. I'm leaving.

[17]

EDITOR: I don't — this is — what? What does this mean?

HANNAH: You hold everyone up so high. You say you love the flaws but you hold everyone up. People don't want to disappoint you.

EDITOR: That's not — I'm — no.

HANNAH: I'm leaving. I've written a book. Maybe I never should have married you.

EDITOR: I can't breathe.

HANNAH: Ben, what can I do? What should I do?

EDITOR: *(Anger and disbelief rising.)* This is why you came down here? To tell me our whole life together was wrong?

HANNAH: In the beginning, I had something else in mind for my life or maybe something else took hold of me and I didn't tell you.

EDITOR: I know you. This isn't true. I know you. What is this book? When did you write a book?

HANNAH: Always. I was always writing a book.

EDITOR: You wrote a book because you shouldn't have married me or — is it filled with love or blame or Hannah, is it — what?

HANNAH: There's love in it. There's love in it. How can you — every book has love in it.

EDITOR: Why can't you write a book and be married to me?

HANNAH: Because I didn't tell you. Because there will be other things I don't tell you.

EDITOR: I don't know what this is.

HANNAH: I wrote a book and there's love in it, but that's not all. There are other things. And I want to write another book with betrayal and ambition and sorrow and disappointment and wreckage.

EDITOR: You wanna leave me, Hannah, for Christ sake come up with a real reason. This is no reason.

HANNAH: It's mine. It's my reason.

EDITOR: Tell me something else. Tell me you're in love with another man. So I can hate someone other than you.

HANNAH: There's no one else. There's no other man.

EDITOR: This is how we end?

HANNAH: I can't be with you right now.

EDITOR: Where are you going? Where are you going so as not to be in this life with me?

HANNAH: Don't corner me, Ben. Don't do that with my words. Don't put your words on my words. Don't cover my meaning.

(He makes an attempt to hold her. She resists with difficulty.)

HANNAH: Please. You could stop me. You could pull me back. Like you do every day. Every day I feel like I'm deciding whether to stay or go. There's always this moment when you have to decide all over again, is this the right thing, is he the right one? Is this the right life?

EDITOR: That's a hell of a way to live, Hannah.

HANNAH: I see the same thing in your eyes. It's there, Ben. It's there and I see it and you know what it is even if you're afraid to know.

EDITOR: Well, I choose you every day. Every day you're my choice.

(Beat.)

I thought our life was a thing that went on. I thought we would continue.

HANNAH: Our life together was everything. It was. I was hopelessly in love with you. But I'm hopeless and you're full of hope.

EDITOR: What, because I see how we are? How humans are. So sure. And then so terribly adrift. We're aflame. Aflame with knowing. And desiring to know. And in a cold panic that there's nothing we'll ever understand. We belong in this together. That's not a mistake. It's exactly what it is.

HANNAH: That first day I looked at you I saw my husband. You're my husband.

EDITOR: Then come home with me.

(A silence. Then DELANEY pops in.)

DELANEY: Excuse me, Ben. You got a call.

EDITOR: Not now.

DELANEY: It's really —

EDITOR: I can't.

DELANEY: You got a call I think you should take.

EDITOR: Hannah —

HANNAH: Forgive me.

(She leaves with great difficulty.)

EDITOR: You're not forgiven. I don't forgive you. I don't know what this is yet!

DELANEY: They're still on the line. They're waiting.

(BEN doesn't respond.)

DELANEY: The call.

EDITOR: *(Hanging on by a thread.)* Yes. All right. No. Can't you — who is it?

DELANEY: Look, just—

EDITOR: Tell them —

DELANEY: Ben, I can't put them off.

(DELANEY puts on the speaker phone.)

DELANEY: I've got Ben Holiday for you. You can go ahead.

EDITOR: I don't — this isn't —

PHONE VOICE: Mr. Holiday?

(BEN doesn't answer.)

PHONE VOICE: Hello? Is this Benjamin Holiday?

(No response.)

Are you there?

EDITOR: I can't talk right now.

PHONE VOICE: I'm calling with good news.

EDITOR: *(Not comprehending.)* I'm sorry — I —

PHONE VOICE: It's my great pleasure to tell you, that you've been awarded a Pulitzer Prize in journalism.

(Beat.)

You there? You there?

EDITOR: *(After an empty moment.)* I'm here.

PHONE VOICE: On behalf of the committee I'd like to extend our heartfelt congratulations.

EDITOR: I don't know what this is. I don't know what this is yet.

(LIGHTS FADE.)

Playing Anne

*(It is 1944. A warm room in a modest house. A young father just
returning from work, has brought home a new movie camera.
His wife, lovely, and anxious. It is clearly the end of the day. She
is dancing to a record which plays the swing/pop music of the era.
Her husband comes through the door, and catches her by surprise.
He takes her into his arms and finishes the dance.)*

DAD: Hey, I've got something.

MOM: You've got something.

DAD: For all of us. I've got something.

MOM: Wait. Just a minute.

DAD: What?

(She kisses him.)

MOM: That.

DAD: I'm pleased and amused.

MOM: *(Acknowledging his distraction.)* But you've got something.

(He takes the camera out of a bag or his briefcase.)

MOM: It's beautiful!

DAD: We'll make a movie.

MOM: Oh, the kids are going to —

DAD: Won't they!

MOM: Well, I don't know about Josie.

DAD: Josie will love this.

MOM: I don't know. She doesn't love anything much these days. Or else she loves things too much. I don't know.

DAD: Well, she's going to love this.

MOM: It's beautiful, though, darling. That you want to.

DAD: Look. Look through here.

(Showing camera.)

It frames everything. Moving. It frames every moving thing. We'll have a movie.

MOM: It's beautiful that you would —

DAD: *(Full of feeling.)* I want us — the family — I want to make a movie of us.

MOM: Josie's not going to — I don't know. Young girls!

DAD: Before it changes. Before she changes. Before Josie —

MOM: *(Enjoying this.)* Young girls are so —

DAD: Yes.

MOM: Aren't they?

DAD: Yes.

MOM: Your collar.

DAD: What?

MOM: Your collar, it's — never mind. It's askew. It's charming.

DAD: Is it?

(Handling the camera.)

This only lasts three minutes. You have to reload. You only get three minutes. It's a beauty, isn't it? It's the newest thing.

MOM: *(A darkening.)* It's just —

DAD: What?

MOM: Something's happening.

DAD: No.

MOM: Your eyes. They cloud over. And —

DAD: No, they don't. They don't cloud over.

MOM: And it frightens me.

DAD: They don't though. Cloud over. I'm —

MOM: Sad or lost.

DAD: Thinking. I'm thinking.

MOM: You're gone.

DAD: I'm just thinking. Probably.

MOM: Not about this.

DAD: I don't have to think about this. I'm here. I'm in this. I'm —

MOM: Something's happening, anyway.

DAD: We're home. We're safe. We're going to make a movie.

(Beat.)

So, let's see. What should everyone do? For the movie. What should everyone be doing?

MOM: We could all walk toward you and wave.

(Beat.)

Or not.

DAD: Why don't you put on that dress.

MOM: What dress?

DAD: The one that moves. The one that kind of swings or —

MOM: I don't have a dress that swings.

DAD: Sways. You do.

MOM: Oh, I know, you mean — the one that — I know.

DAD: Will you?

MOM: All right.

(Starts to go, then turns.)

DAD: *(Almost startled by this.)* What?

MOM: Do you remember —

DAD: Everything.

MOM: I mean — do you remember — just one thing?

(He is stunned by this. After a moment, she turns and leaves to change into the dress. JOSIE, their twelve-year-old daughter comes into the room.)

DAD: There she is. There's the one.

JOSIE: I feel sort of dreamy.

DAD: You are sort of dreamy. You are.

JOSIE: I wonder about —

DAD: About?

JOSIE: I just wonder. You and Mom.

DAD: Oh.

JOSIE: You and Mom.

DAD: We're — what?

JOSIE: I don't know.

DAD: Well, we're okay. We're —

JOSIE: No, not that.

DAD: Sometimes. Now, sometimes. Two people. Two people are always —

JOSIE: What if something happens?

DAD: Look what I brought home.

JOSIE: I don't want my picture taken.

DAD: It'll be good.

JOSIE: I don't want —

DAD: What's the — why don't you — what's the—

JOSIE: I'll see it one day and I won't understand. I won't be the same and I won't understand how I was. Before. On the day you —

DAD: That's with photographs. This is a movie. Someday you'll be glad to have this.

JOSIE: I won't. I'll be unhappy.

DAD: You can bet Myrna Loy is happy.

JOSIE: She's a movie star.

DAD: You can bet Myrna Loy and your pal Claudette Colbert are happy.

JOSIE: You don't make any sense, Daddy. Really.

DAD: They are two happy gals. I'm sure of it.

JOSIE: They have words. To speak.

DAD: You can have words. Give yourself words.

JOSIE: What would I say?

(A YOUNG BOY, *Josie's younger brother, calls out from another room: "Daddy!"*)

DAD: He wants his glass of water.

JOSIE: He's not even thirsty.

DAD: I know.

JOSIE: He just wants —

DAD: I know.

JOSIE: I'm bored of having a brother today.

DAD: I'll just bring him a glass of water.

JOSIE: He isn't even thirsty.

DAD: He wants me to bring it to him, that's all.

JOSIE: And then he'll ask you to line up his shoes.

DAD: He wants order. I have to make order for him. And then I'll be back.

(*He makes a small move, as if to leave the room.*)

JOSIE: *(Urgent.)* Daddy! Dad!

DAD: Josie!

(*As if to say, what is it? What in the world is it?*)

JOSIE: Just. Sometimes —

DAD: Josie!

JOSIE: Just. Sometimes I miss you.

DAD: I'm right here.

JOSIE: I miss you though. Terribly.

DAD: I'm here.

JOSIE: Just sometimes. I think you'll go.

DAD: I won't go. I'll never go.

JOSIE: Then why do I see things without you? Without you there. You aren't there.

DAD: You'll go, sweetie. You're the one. You'll go.

JOSIE: I imagine you in your car and I imagine an accident. I practice it. My mind practices you gone. You walk out the door, out of my room. And I can't smell you. All I want to do is smell you.

DAD: *(Moved.)* Well, I'm sure no one's ever — ever — said such a thing.

JOSIE: And touch the hem of Mom's dress. Like she does.

DAD: She does. She does that. Well, you're just the most alarming child. You're going to be a great person, Josie. You're going to do something fine.

JOSIE: Will I?

DAD: I know it.

JOSIE: Does everyone have a lot of thoughts at once? I have a lot of thoughts at once. I don't know if I'm supposed to have so many. So many at once.

DAD: Let me see your head.

(He touches her head. As if to examine it.)

Perfectly normal head.

JOSIE: It's too big. It's bigger than almost all my friends.

DAD: The movie stars have big heads. It's a sign of something. Well — big.

JOSIE: *(A sudden happiness.)* I'm going to make a movie of all the rooms in the house!

(She takes the camera and begins to shoot as she moves out of the room. He sits for a moment. Gets up. Pours a drink. His WIFE appears. Wearing a dress.)

DAD: The dress! Turn around. Turn around for me.

(She turns.)

DAD: See. It swirls.

MOM: *(Playfully.)* You said it swung.

DAD: Well, I was wrong.

MOM: Sometimes I could almost stop breathing.

DAD: Everything's all right.

MOM: From joy. From so much fear and joy.

(Beat.)

I just want to keep everyone.

DAD: Hey, come here. You with the dress.

(JOSIE appears, with the camera.)

MOM: Put it down, Josie. My hair. Put it down.

DAD: You're lovely.

MOM: I'm tangled. I'm in disarray.

DAD: I like that about you.

(JOSIE points the camera at various things in the room as she speaks.)

JOSIE: Here's our kitchen. And here is a bright wall. And here are two people leaning in the doorway. And there is a window. And a striped light from the venetian blinds makes my mother's face — romantic.

(A sudden shift.)

No, don't look at the camera. You're looking too hard. You're looking too hard at the camera. You have to look at each other.

MOM: It's time for supper, Jo. It's time to put it down now.

DAD: Let her. She's fine. Let her.

MOM: You are both — you know you are both —

(Enjoying them — enjoying giving over to them.)

All right, where should I look, Jo? Tell me where to look.

JOSIE: At your darling man.

MOM: *(Laughing.)* At my darling man. Okay. I'm looking.

DAD: Should I look back at her, Josie? Or —

JOSIE: I don't know. I don't know. I just wanted it to be —

MOM: *(Trying to comfort.)* Come on, Josie. Come on sweetie, we're — see!

JOSIE: *(A plaintive cry.)* Oh, don't. Don't. Don't. Don't die.

(Lights fade on this area. The same actors we just saw as JOSIE and DAD change spaces to become the characters in this next scene. Lights up on another small part of the stage. An attic room, familiar. With a window. A young GIRL, in a sweater with a roughly sewn on yellow Jewish star, stands looking out the window. She has been looking through a pair of binoculars, watching the family in the house across the street. After a moment, her FATHER walks in.)

MR. FRANK: What is it, Anne?

ANNE: Nothing.

MR. FRANK: You were looking at something through the binoculars.

ANNE: I'm sorry, Pim. I couldn't help myself.

MR. FRANK: *(Weary. Tired of imposing rules.)* It's all right.

ANNE: Sometimes —

MR. FRANK: I know.

ANNE: I'm sorry.

MR. FRANK: Tell me. What did you see?

ANNE: Just a family. They were making a movie.

(Lights change. And we hear a VOICE, *saying "Can we try that again?"* JOSIE, *now a grown woman, is standing in the Annex Room Set with the* ACTRESS *playing "Anne." It becomes clear that what we just saw was a scene being shot as a movie, which* JOSIE *is directing.)*

GIRL: I'm sorry. I was — .

JOSIE: No, it's lovely. You're so close.

GIRL: I don't know. It doesn't feel right. I want to do it justice.

JOSIE: *(Warmly, to* ACTOR *playing Mr. Frank.)* Can you just give us a minute?

ACTOR: Sure.

(He walks off.)

JOSIE: You're just standing at the window. You're standing and looking.

GIRL: Am I sad? Or —

JOSIE: You're just looking. You're looking out the window.

GIRL: I have to work from some emotion, Josie.

JOSIE: Say the words. It's the rhythm of that. And how you're standing and just looking. It'll give you what you need.

GIRL: I'm looking. I'm standing. All right.

JOSIE: And your father walks in. And he sees what you're doing. This is against all the house rules. This is forbidden. But he's so tired. He's so tired of imposing rules.

GIRL: And he catches the wonder in his daughter's voice.

JOSIE: Yes!

GIRL: What are those people doing? In the next house?

JOSIE: They're making a movie.

GIRL: I know. But what do I see exactly?

JOSIE: It doesn't matter. It's simple. They're together. They have the lights on. They eat a meal. They argue. They throw open a window. It doesn't matter.

GIRL: But, doesn't everything matter?

JOSIE: Well, yes, but not how you think.

GIRL: I want to be good in this, Jo.

JOSIE: You will be. If you can stand at the window and not know how it turns out. You're just a young girl. Nobody's made you into something. Nobody's read your diary. You don't belong to the world yet. You're not everyone's "Anne Frank."

(Lights fade on this scene, as a movie screen comes down. JOSIE walks in front of it and sits on a chair across from a MAN who is interviewing her.)

INTERVIEWER: So, what did you know? What did you know then?

JOSIE: What do you know at 12? I knew something. That I'd be separate. I knew it was all going to end. The family. The family was going to end. Someday, there wouldn't be any comfort. I'd lose my place in it. I didn't know why. Then this wave of — loss. This wave of knowing — of parting. It took me. I couldn't eat. I couldn't — well, and then I sort of started to revel in it. I was a young girl, after all.

INTERVIEWER: Yes. But what did you know in 1944? About the Jews. The Jews in Europe? About her — about Anne Frank?

JOSIE: That's the year I was born. I was born the year she was found and taken to the camps.

INTERVIEWER: But, you place the family in that year. In your film, isn't Josie — aren't you — ?

JOSIE: I put myself at her age. Every Jewish girl when you get to be twelve or thirteen you think, that's how old she was. In 1944 my mother was pregnant with me. My father was in the army. I just changed the order of things. Years after the war, he brought me a camera. And I thought, what if it had been 1944. To depict what it would be like to just be having an ordinary day where all you care about, all you're doing is trying to make sense of your household. That's all you know. You don't know what's going on anywhere except what's happening to you, in the rooms of your own house.

(Beat.)

But, that's what it's like, isn't it? That's what's going on every-where. In one house, there's supper. A brother taunts his sister. In the doorway of the kitchen your mother says, "I don't un-derstand," and your father turns away. He catches his children looking at him and lifts them into the air. This is happening in one house. And in another there's slaughter.

INTERVIEWER: By showing the rehearsal — the rehearsal of the attic scene, by leaving this in the film — by inserting yourself into the picture, as it were, were you saying—

JOSIE: It just happened. I liked it. I liked that it —

INTERVIEWER: It gives you a kind of, I mean, the feeling of the audience, I think is that you create a kind of —

JOSIE: I liked that it was a mistake. A mistake that if you try to correct, you maybe lose the thing that was true about it.

INTERVIEWER: So, tell us something, Josie, in making this film, what were you trying to resolve?

JOSIE: I don't — what do you —

INTERVIEWER: In terms of —

JOSIE: In terms of ?

INTERVIEWER: Well, can we say then, that a young girl stands there with her father's camera. Something's revealed. Something's shattered. And nobody knows what's going on anywhere else but in their own house.

JOSIE: You know, I think I said too much.

INTERVIEWER: Talk to me about the audition sequence and why it's never been shown.

JOSIE: It's really no mystery. I cut it.

INTERVIEWER: You cut it. Uh huh. You had no pressure to — I understood that you — but, you're saying you had no pressure to —

JOSIE: I decided it wasn't —

INTERVIEWER: Oh, I understood that — well, anyhow, some people saw it. Obviously. Some people who thought —

JOSIE: It didn't work, that's all.

INTERVIEWER: Could you — tell us.

JOSIE: *(After a reluctant moment.)* There's an audition. A group of girls waiting to audition. For a play. They're typically modern. In attitude and dress. And among them sits this dark haired girl. You don't notice her right away. They don't notice her. Her clothes are period, sort of shabby, but could be mistaken for a sense of style and a vintage look. She's got a star sewn on to the sweater she wears over her dress. The talk is all "Borrow your lipstick," "My mother's such a bitch," "Do you have Mr. Lane for English?" A party. A date. Does he like me? Does anyone like me? While the real Anne Frank sits among them. Then one of them notices the girl and the yellow star. And says, "That's so cool. I should've thought of that. That's so genius."

(Beat.)

She's come because she hopes this will be a production she can bless, a production that is magnificent. She comes to watch over the other girls. To —

(Her words fall off.)

—anyhow.

INTERVIEWER: And, what, you — it didn't work? You —

JOSIE: Look. Look. I didn't want to put so much on these young girls. Nobody believes what happens to other people. Nobody is there for the reason that we want to really know. We think that's why. I mean, of course, we think that's why. I didn't want to put these young girls in the wrong light. To say they're callow or vapid. They're having their modern life. They'll know some things but not this. I wanted Anne, the real Anne, to shed her clothes, to let them see her shorn head, her hunger, her loss, her end. But, nobody can do that. Nobody can see it.

INTERVIEWER: *(Beat.)* So, what's next for you?

(Movie screen goes up. Lights shift. JOSIE *and* INTEVIEWER *leave. Two* FILM ENTHUSIASTS *who were in the audience for the screening of Josie's film and her interview, sit at a small table in "the Cafe" with their espressos.)*

MAN 2: Okay, but, what you're saying — I mean, if I'm seeing it the way you see it — which I'm not saying I do, necessarily, but why do you think —

MAN 1: Because it has all the elements.

MAN 2: All the elements.

MAN 1: It's modern. It's the modern moment. A girls' diary. It's how we know something happened. Confession. And witness. I mean, you can look at the 20th Century a couple of ways. The bomb. And the movies.

MAN 2: And the personal memoir.

MAN 1: Right. Yes. Yes, because a person wants to know his place in it. A person turning 30, 40, wants to know. Gets religion, goes back to the old neighborhood, contacts relatives. Maybe school chums. A person loses a father and it's all down the road of who am I now. Who am I without him. And then a person will think what right do I have, what's personal mourning? What right? And you start down the road of look what happened. Look what happened in the world. But you have this personal grief. And you are either going to be someone who — who rescues children or you are going to be caught up in your personal grief. You are going to be caught up and trying to make sense of why you were spared from what happened in the world to everyone else.

MAN 2: Why not me.

MAN 1: You never make sense of it. You go on to other things.

(Screen comes down again and lights come up on the area with screen behind it.

This should be seen with a subtle flickering light or camera sound to indicate it is part of a film.—Josie's film. THREE WOMEN *sit on stools and talk directly ahead, as if to audience.)*

ACTRESS 1: I played Anne in high school.

ACTRESS 2: I was Anne in the first road company in Philadelphia. My agents sent me up for the movie. I wasn't Jewish or anything. I told them, I think she's gotta be Jewish. You know. But they said, this is not your concern. Role of a lifetime. I got a screen test. Ended up as a stand in for Miss Perkins. That's where you have the hot lights on you and everything.

ACTRESS 1: Then I did Anne for my Yale audition. Which everyone said are you crazy? Which is like against the trend. I mean, I know. There was everyone else doing Nellie Forbush from Anne Bogart's "South Pacific."

ACTRESS 2: Well, it was a turning point for me. In that, I gave up acting after that.

ACTRESS 3: I was doing the speech about the mean Anne and the good Anne. For my audition. And I caught the look in the director's face. And I said, I'm not gonna get this part, am I? "All due respect," he tells me. "All due respect, but —" But I'm a young girl. And this is the diary of a young girl. And I'm a young girl. Like she was. And old like she was, too. Nobody else here except me is old like she was. He says, "Are we gonna have a situation?" See a thing happens or doesn't happen just because I'm black. That's the situation. See, and that's how I'm a Jew. That's how I can be her.

(Lights fade. Screen goes up. WOMEN *leave.)*

(Lights up on Cafe. The FILM ENTHUSIASTS *we saw earlier are sitting at one table. The* EDITOR *sits at another with coffee and a newspaper.* JOSIE *sits at the table next to him. The same song which Josie's mother danced to when she was young, plays in the background. The* EDITOR, *lost like a man who's wife has left him, distractedly hums or sings a few words.)*

JOSIE: You know this song? I can never remember the words.

EDITOR: You're here for the — thing. The —

JOSIE: *(Nods.)* Mmm.

EDITOR: The coffee. They make it stronger when everyone's in town for the —

JOSIE: Festival.

EDITOR: The coffee gets stronger.

JOSIE: Do you think people can recover from anything?

(Beat.)

(Conversation from the other table:)

MAN 1: The part where the actresses — the ones who played her — where they talk about —

MAN 2: The ones who played her?

MAN 1: The ones who — right. Where they talk about I was in this production, I was in that — don't you think —

MAN 2: Wait. Were they actresses? I mean, were they playing actresses who played her or —

MAN 1: It was documentary. At that point.

MAN 2: It was. I thought it was. But then.

MAN 1: It doesn't matter, really.

MAN 2: She seemed reluctant to talk about her new one.

MAN 1: I hear it's completely not personal.

MAN 2: Oh, really? Her new one. Where did you hear that?

MAN 1: Oh. No. Actually, I didn't hear that. I was thinking of someone else. But, if you listen to everything she said, that's what you'd take away. That's what I took away.

(Beat.)

I love this song.

(Picking up the conversation between JOSIE *and* EDITOR.*)*

JOSIE: I was having an interview and he asked me, he said at the end, "What is the sound you love?" Then, "What is the sound you hate?"

EDITOR: Excuse me. You're the filmmaker?

JOSIE: Yes

EDITOR: I'm the husband.

JOSIE: You're the husband?

EDITOR: In the book. I'm the husband.

(Beat.)

I understand you're turning my wife's book into a movie.

JOSIE: You're Harry?

EDITOR: That's what she's calling me.

JOSIE: You're Harry.

EDITOR: I'm Ben. She's stolen my shortcomings and given them to a guy named Harry.

JOSIE: You could look at it as a — kind of gift.

EDITOR: Has anyone turned you into literature?

JOSIE: She made you a character. I mean, now you have a destiny. A rise and fall. Harry's flaws are dynamic. They have meaning here.

EDITOR: You're saying as a real person my flaws are not so beautiful.

JOSIE: Anyway, aren't you a writer? Harry's a writer. So, Harry knows about turning other people's lives to his own purpose.

EDITOR: Why do you want to make Hannah's book into a movie?

JOSIE: Because it's about someone my age. It's about how someone got to be my age. I've been looking for such a long time at a girl who never got older. But, the girl in the book, she grows up. She gets older. She makes mistakes.

EDITOR: I'm only on Chapter Six. I've been on Chapter Six for a long time. I can't face how it ends.

JOSIE: Don't you know how it ends?

(Beat.)

Listen, you don't have to worry about Harry. I'll be kind. Anyway, it's really the woman's story.

EDITOR: Which is the man's story if only he paid attention.

JOSIE: Which is everyone's story.

EDITOR: This is *my* divorce. This is my heartbreak. It's about the end of things for me!

JOSIE: You should really finish the book.

EDITOR: What she says I said on page 33, I didn't say. I never said that.

JOSIE: All right.

EDITOR: I would never say that.

JOSIE: If you say so.

EDITOR: Well, I didn't mean it.

(Beat.)

I didn't know she was writing a book. How could I not know?

JOSIE: We don't know what we're looking at most of the time.

EDITOR: *(Silently acknowledging.)* One of the films they're showing in the —

JOSIE: Festival.

EDITOR: Well, the projectionist, he's a local guy, good man, got the reels mixed up. Played the end in the middle. So, he's down. He's beating himself up about it. And I'm drawn to his situation. Now when I see him, I'm delicate.

JOSIE: That's sweet. That's good.

EDITOR: You think I'm sweet and good. You think I just carry people in my heart out of goodness? The only way I see that man at all is because most of my life he had nothing to say to me. He didn't matter. Then one day I'm caught. I'm apprehended in my self absorption. I catch the wounded expression in a good person's eyes and I understand — for the first time, really — people see you. People see you not looking.

JOSIE: I liked how your friend put the end where it didn't belong. Things got much more interesting that way. You can tell him that for me. He did everyone a favor.

EDITOR: What kind of a man are you going to show me to be?

JOSIE: You really should ask what kind of person am I. Given our man, Harry, is in my hands.

EDITOR: What kind of person *are* you? I'm at a disadvantage. Unless you have an ex husband somewhere who's written a book.

JOSIE: It could happen. I could have an ex. If — well, anyhow, she's a doctor. She's beyond the personal. She'll never tell. What do you want to know?

EDITOR: Why do you think it might not last?

JOSIE: Sometimes there aren't any reasons. Or any reasons you can actually give to someone who asks. Much as you'd like to.

EDITOR: I think if a man could be a young girl for just one minute in his life he would know the answer to all things.

JOSIE: I was a young girl. It's a total mystery.

(Beat.)

My . . . doctor. She's in the world. She's not attempting to make a world. You know? She's the bigger thing. She looks someone over and says this is what it is. This is what I can do. She's not asking anyone in pain to appreciate the symbolic. She brings what relief she can directly to the ache. She is face to face with another person's utterly private declarations. And if she can't help, at least she doesn't cause confusion. Which is what I can do. Cause chagrin and confusion.

(Beat.)

Well, so, I really fell for her. It was at the animal medical center. She was there with her dog. I was there to *observe* people with their dogs. And she said, I really admire them, the vets. Because they'll never know what the animal is really feeling or thinking. They have to have a kind of faith and acceptance that they'll never know if what they're doing is right or helpful or understood. It's so purely human. *(Beat.)* Like you. She told me later. Like what you do.

(A moment.)

EDITOR: How *does* the book end?

JOSIE: It's not so much how it ends —

EDITOR: I'd like the chance to make it come out differently.

JOSIE: So would I. *(Letting the music in.)* This song. My father taught me to dance to this song.

EDITOR: Did he do the jitterbug or the box step? Your father. Was it swing or — here —

(He demonstrates the steps. She is charmed.)

JOSIE: I think the box step.

(He puts out his hand to her. She gets up and repeats his movements. They dance, enjoying it.

Then sit down again.)

JOSIE: There's never going to be another song like this.

EDITOR: Maybe we don't need another one of what we already have. Someone's going to write another song. Someone will come along and give us another good thing.

JOSIE: Okay, but, what happens to the thing that's never invented or dreamed of or found because people died before they should have? Where are their creations?

EDITOR: We're their creations. I mean, everything we do is — is — their absence, it's part of our condition. It's who we are.

JOSIE: Do you have children? Of course. Harry. Harry's a father.

EDITOR: And you?

JOSIE: I have a son.

(Then, with a knowledge of all that's come apart in the world.)

How did *we* get to keep our children? How?

(Lights up on 1944 Living Room. We hear the sound of a film reel under the following: YOUNG JOSIE *stands by the window, where she's been filming. Her* DAD *comes in. Josie puts down the camera, her face, transfixed.)*

YOUNG JOSIE: I saw someone. At the window. A girl.

DAD: Come away, Jo.

YOUNG JOSIE: She was looking at me.

DAD: Time for bed.

YOUNG JOSIE: She was looking at me.

(Lights fade.)

END OF ACT ONE

Act Two

ACT TWO

The End of Disaster

Lights up on JOSIE *in her hotel room, in the town where the film festival was held. In the immediate aftermath of a hurricane that's hit the town. She's on her cell with her lover.*

JOSIE: Babe, are you there? No, I'm all right. But, I can't get out. The roads are closed. Everything's down. They won't let anyone leave the hotel. I don't know what's going on. It's bad. Talk to me before I lose you again.

While lights remain on JOSIE, *lights come up on the Cafe, which has been turned into a temporary shelter for people in the town. The scene should shift seamlessly between the hotel room and the shelter throughout. People mill about. A* VOLUNTEER *comes in and out, bearing food, coffee, and other necessary things. His arms are loaded with blankets. He speaks to* RACHEL, *a young woman who's also brought something she thinks might be necessary. She is appealing and slightly awkward.*

VOLUNTEER: I'm just saying — it's too soon, maybe. It's too soon for this.

RACHEL: I just thought —

VOLUNTEER: No. Go ahead. You should. You should.

RACHEL: Because I was thinking it was — really?

VOLUNTEER: When people are wondering how to get home. That's all. No, but. You should.

RACHEL moves into the room, tosses off her large knapsack, looks at everyone gathered here. As she removes some art reproductions from her bag.

RACHEL: I know this is a hard time and all, but — I just want to — I had this idea — oh, I'm Rachel. And — well, I just wanted to show you some things. Some pictures. That some artists did.

(In Hotel:)

JOSIE: *(On phone.)* I'm trying to work. I'm trying to concentrate. If I start thinking about what's happening to everyone, I'll lose it. So, humor me. I'm having trouble with the last scene. Have you finished it yet? Okay, well read the last sentence.

(Beat.)

Because last sentences are important. How could you not know that? I don't want this film to be just a story about one couple coming apart. It's larger than that. It's how another person puts you in touch with the world. *(Beat.)* You see us in it? Uh huh. In what way?

(Beat.)

Maybe that's why I'm having such a hard time working on it.

(Beat.)

Look, the way we left things — I'm — you know how I get before I go away.

(Beat.)

What do you mean? How has it taken a toll?

(Losing connection.)

Oh god, I'm losing you.

(In Shelter:)

RACHEL: The pictures. I thought it could be a good thing. To — well, to have this. To have something like this to look at.

Because — I mean, something a person made out of nothing, out of the air, a thing like that can remind you. A thing like that, out of nothing, just one person's mind or hands or seeing. It can — *art* can — I thought —

(Beat.)

You know?

(She props up a Cezanne against the wall or chair.)

RACHEL: *(Determinedly upbeat.)* Okay. Like, here's a peach and a jar on a table. And this peach and this jar on this table. This fruit. This wood. This color. Is all. Is enough to —

SEYMOUR: I had a picture. Of my wife. We were on vacation. And we had a fight. She was unhappy because I paid too much attention to a pretty girl at dinner, she said. I was happy. I was excited by my wife. To be with her. I liked the pretty girl because she chattered on and it made me want my wife more. It was a secret I was having while I talked to the girl. I was flushed. I was imagining later. I was thinking of soap. And my wife's neck. And the inside of her thighs. She threw a book at me. Hemingway. No, Fitzgerald. I laughed so hard.

VOLUNTEER: *(Walking over with big bag.)* I don't know what's exactly in here. Clothes. Warm things.

WINNIE: Shoes, I hope.

SEYMOUR: Anything. We appreciate anything you've got.

RACHEL: Would you like some books? I could bring you some books. I've got Hemingway. Oh, no, you said Fitzgerald. Well, I've got some books if anyone —

WINNIE: Some fabulous shoes.

GIRL: Do you have any Nancy Drew books?

WINNIE: Oh. I used to read her. Do they still write those? I used to enjoy those. She had a shiny roadster.

SEYMOUR: There's mud in my bed. There is mud in my chair and my bed. You can't think of love when there's that.

(In Hotel:)

JOSIE: What's going on? Something's going on. Dammit, I know there's an emergency. We're having an emergency. You and me. And you can't help anyone else right now and neither can I. So, just — help me — understand what's going on.

(Beat.)

All right. Maybe I do. Maybe I do always have one foot out the door. Because something could come and tear it asunder. I see it all around me. So, I'm always ready, that's all. It doesn't mean that —

(The phone connection starts to go.)

Are you there?

(In Shelter, the GIRL *addresses the* VOLUNTEER:)

GIRL: Did you find a dog?

VOLUNTEER: I'm sorry. Not yet. I'm sorry.

WINNIE: Were there any animals? Did any of the animals —

VOLUNTEER: Not yet.

WINNIE: I can't stand thinking about if my dog is — he's so good and all. He's so sweet and good.

RACHEL: You know, dogs, sometimes they come back. They want to come back. They try so hard.

(In Hotel:)

JOSIE: Honey, listen to me. What I said before I left. It was hypo-thetical. It was a hypothetical conversation. Who would get what "if." I didn't mean to start us down a terrible path. I don't care whose albums are whose. I'll never read another book or listen to show music again if we break up. I want us to be happy.

(The connection starts breaking up.)

Can you hear me? How can I tell you everything I need to tell you if you can't hear me?

(In Shelter:)

RACHEL: Would you like to see another one?

(Braving on, RACHEL *takes out a Matisse and puts it on display.)*

SEYMOUR: I'm still thinking about that peach. I'd like to take a bite out of that peach.

WINNIE: *(Looking at painting.)* Everyone seems — in the painting — to be — everyone seems — like it's before everything. Before things.

RACHEL: *(Thrilled to have a response.)* You see that! I saw that, too. Well, I mean, you don't know what an artist had in mind. You don't know for sure.

GIRL: I think it means something. But I don't want everyone to talk about it.

*(*SEYMOUR *has walked over to the coffeepot.)*

SEYMOUR: I just forgot why I walked over here.

VOLUNTEER: That happens to me. I go into a room. I don't know what I'm there for.

SEYMOUR: The thing I can't seem to — you're on a street. You're on a street in a city. You're located. You're on the South Side or someplace. You're in the neighborhood. You have an address. The thing I can't —

GIRL: We live on Wyoming Street.

SEYMOUR: I don't know that street.

WINNIE: Over there by the stationery supplies. Over by Gennaro's.

SEYMOUR: Gennaro's. You get a terrific Italian hoagie there. With peppers. They don't hold back. They give you everything.

WINNIE: They lost their daughter. She was so attractive. She was an attractive girl.

SEYMOUR: They didn't lose their daughter.

WINNIE: Well, she went. She went away somewhere.

SEYMOUR: Turned gay.

WINNIE: They were very polite.

SEYMOUR: What good is that? What good is that to the girl? You have a daughter, she's yours. She's always yours.

VOLUNTEER: I think it was the coffee.

SEYMOUR: What?

VOLUNTEER: Why you walked over here. You were going for the coffee.

WINNIE: You know Ruthie Sacco's dance studio?

GIRL: I know Ruthie.

WINNIE: She's a winning personality. She just lights up a room.

GIRL: A lot of kids take tap from Ruthie.

WINNIE: I took tap from Ruthie. I 'd do the steps in my head. You know, the combinations. She said I had some moves. It made life very upbeat.

SEYMOUR: I mean, how do people reach you? Where does it put you in the world? You were always somewhere. You could be located. You have no porch or steps. You're off the map.

WINNIE: I used to see you out there. On the porch. You had a nice green awning.

SEYMOUR: It was nice, wasn't it?

WINNIE: Green and white striped.

SEYMOUR: Yes. Green and white striped.

WINNIE: It always gave me a summertime feeling. It was fresh. It always made me a little sad, though.

SEYMOUR: We didn't invite you over. Why didn't we?

WINNIE: That's all right.

SEYMOUR: No.

WINNIE: We weren't friends.

(In Hotel:)

JOSIE: *(On phone, with bad connection.)* I'm going to say this. Even if you can't hear me saying it.

(Beat.)

I want us to be together. You encourage me. I'm comforted and encouraged by you. Your mail. Your magazines. Your coffee cup. I need those things to know that I'm here. That I'm in the world. That I'm not just looking at it. That I'm in it with everyone else. I want to be in it. I want us to last.

(Beat.)

I hope you heard. I hope you know.

(In Shelter, RACHEL *puts up another painting.)*

RACHEL: Do you know Hockney? Well, here's this picture of what seems to be — what seems to be —well, here are these chairs. These chairs around a pool. This gorgeous life. With a Picasso mural behind it. And you think — they have a good situation. Whoever owns the chairs and the mural and the pool. And then. Then, a child falls into the pool. Or — what I'm saying is — or, in the next moment, an earthquake. A fire. You look at this and you say, such a gorgeous life, but, you don't know if — if before, before the chairs and the pool, if everything was lost. If this is just the attempt to — the attempt to —

(To the GIRL.*)*

Could you draw your dog? Your dog, could you? I have some — wait — I have some pencils. Some colored pencils.

GIRL: Do you have Burnt Sienna?

(RACHEL roots in her bag to retrieve pencils and paper, which she gives to the GIRL.)

SEYMOUR: This person, Hockney or whoever, if we don't know what he's thinking, it kind of makes fools out of us, doesn't it?

VOLUNTEER: I think what she's saying is —

SEYMOUR: Because I don't need that.

VOLUNTEER: What she might be saying is, that not knowing what it's supposed to mean is almost the best part. Not knowing for sure. Because, anyhow, the picture doesn't mean anything without someone looking at it. It's like you sort of don't need the painter anymore. But the painting needs you.

(Beat.)

Anyhow, I think that's what she's saying.

SEYMOUR: Are you from New York?

VOLUNTEER: You mean — well, from, no. I'm — from — well, but I live there. So, I guess I am. From.

SEYMOUR: People from New York show up with that confidence about them.

VOLUNTEER: What it is, is, all these strangers you gotta put your trust with. Like how easy a cab driver could kidnap you. But he takes you where you're going. You're so glad to have your life back, you wanna do right by someone else. I don't think it's so much we're confident as we're grateful, you know. I don't know.

(He walks off.)

RACHEL: I tried to live there. I'm going to try it again.

WINNIE: There's a lot of disappointment in New York.

SEYMOUR: But not too much mud.

(He laughs at his own joke.)

RACHEL: I still live here, though. I live right here.

SEYMOUR: Not much mud at all.

RACHEL: My house — I can go back. Only, there used to be a house next to me. Before. I could look out my kitchen window and there it was. I can go back. Except — my house needs that other house. Or I'm not home.

VOLUNTEER: I made a fresh pot of coffee. If anyone — well, it's made.

(In Hotel, JOSIE has just regained her connection:)

JOSIE: Oh, thank god. You're there.

(Beat.)

Have coffee with me. Yes, right now. Let's have coffee together. Because what if we don't have another morning?

(Thinking of the worst scenario, but not wanting to say it.)

If it all goes, I want to know we're having a morning.

(In Shelter:)

WINNIE: I need to call someone. They'll be worried. We all need to call someone.

VOLUNTEER: Yes. Soon. Hopefully. Just —

SEYMOUR: *(To* WINNIE.*)* We should've been friends. We were almost – you don't know who I am, do you? I was a year behind you in high school. I asked you out. I asked you out on a date.

WINNIE: You never asked me on a date.

SEYMOUR: I had more hair then.

WINNIE: You never asked me out. You didn't go to my high school.

SEYMOUR: You were walking down the hall one day. And you looked so above it all. I mean in a good way. Like you were going places.

WINNIE: I was going to be a nurse. I was going away to school.

SEYMOUR: You smiled at me. You probably smiled at everyone. But you smiled at me and I took it for myself. And I asked you out.

GIRL: What did she say? When you asked her out? What did you say?

SEYMOUR: She said "Call me."

WINNIE: But we never went.

SEYMOUR: I didn't call. My friends said I was crazy for asking, you'd never go, you were just being — so I never called. In the hall it seemed possible.

WINNIE: I didn't finish school. I got homesick. I could have gotten so much out of it.

(Beat.)

You should've called.

GIRL: What if he called and you went out on a date and you got married. And then you fell out of love and got divorced. You'd feel terrible now.

VOLUNTEER: I just got engaged. She's a great girl. I think it's gonna last.

WINNIE: *(To the* GIRL.*)* Didn't I see you in that school play? That play about the diary. Didn't you play that Jewish girl?

GIRL: Anne Frank.

WINNIE: You were her! That was you! You did a good job. All you kids. You were so professional.

GIRL: Really? You think?

WINNIE: I could never get up on a stage. I'd be so nervous. How did you remember all those words? You didn't forget any. Not that I could tell. I'd be so nervous. You had me crying, too.

SEYMOUR: We'll rebuild. We'll get the money and we'll rebuild.

WINNIE: Do you want to be an actress when you grow up? You were so natural out there. You positively shone.

GIRL: I want to be a writer.

WINNIE: Oh. A writer. What kind of writer? You gonna write stories? You gonna write about us? Look out!

SEYMOUR: Then someone can throw your books at me. I'd be proud.

WINNIE: Write a story where nothing bad happens. Write a story like that.

GIRL: All right.

(Beat.)

There'll be a dog in it. And a painting. A dog and a painting and a book.

WINNIE: And a kiss?

SEYMOUR: Now! She doesn't have to put kisses in.

WINNIE: I think there's always a kiss, though. Kisses are always there.

SEYMOUR: All right. All right. A kiss then.

WINNIE: A story where someone sits on a porch and no one comes to take them away and there's a breeze and no one hurts them. There's a cool breeze and a kiss.

SEYMOUR: It's morning.

(In Hotel:)

JOSIE: It's morning. It's the beginning of the day. We're starting.

(In Shelter:)

SEYMOUR: Everything is starting.

WINNIE: And nothing bad happens.

SEYMOUR: There's a porch. And a breeze and a conversation. And nothing bad will ever happen again.

RACHEL: This was — I thought if I — I thought when I brought the — but, really, it's just not what people need. Is it?

SEYMOUR: Are you an artist? I'll bet you're an artist, aren't you?

RACHEL: Oh, no. I mean, I paint. But, it's hard to call myself — well, anything. I thought if art could be consoling, if it could —

SEYMOUR: Do you have one of yours to show us? I'd like to see something of yours.

RACHEL: Mine were — well, I lost a lot of my stuff.

(Beat.)

I have an idea, though. Wait. You gave me an idea for something. Maybe it will be the best thing I've ever done.

WINNIE: I never got around to putting my photographs in an album. They were in shoeboxes. In the basement.

SEYMOUR: I have one. This one I carry in my wallet. My wallet's survived Vietnam, the collapse of Russia. Well, I wasn't there in Russia, I mean, but you feel all these reverberations. Don't you?

(He pulls the photograph out.)

That's my father there leaning on a car. A young man, with his white shirt sleeves rolled up and suspenders and a shock of white hair. He had a streak of white hair up the middle. My father pulled my cousin out of a moving car. He ran up and pulled him out the window. Saved his life. I don't know what for exactly.

(The photograph is now passed along. Each person looks at the photo, commenting as if it were actually one of their own.)

GIRL: My mother has my brother and sister and me all dressed alike. All corny and alike. In plaid. My brother and me we're okay with it, but my sister is crying. Her arms out and crying.

WINNIE: This was on our honeymoon, that town in — look at us! We were so —

RACHEL: Noni. Noni, I used to call her. She taught me the alphabet.

SEYMOUR: A week before he died.

WINNIE: V.E Day. My father is celebrating. In his undershorts. All tan and — I have to look away.

SEYMOUR: He always thought he'd see his parents again. Afterwards. I like to think of him that way. With them.

WINNIE: The day I mixed up the laundry and turned my husband's underwear pink. I thought it was the end of the world. He wore his pink underwear to work the next day. Smiling. He made me take his picture.

(In Hotel:)

JOSIE: *(Also referring to a photograph.)* The one we took in the photo booth. You still have it? Really. What you were doing to me.

(In Shelter:)

GIRL: Say cheese! My mother is trying so hard. We're not happy here. We never got as happy as she wanted us to be.

SEYMOUR: A Brooklyn dodger game. Sandy Koufax was pitching. I wore this little baseball uniform. Everyone on the subway said hello to me. I thought they all knew me.

WINNIE: She's black and blue. Her lip is swollen. She's hurt. Some-one hurt her. Her boyfriend. I didn't recognize her. I thought it was someone else's child. It can't be your own child. You wouldn't let anything happen to your own child.

SEYMOUR: I remember.

WINNIE: I can see it.

RACHEL: I remember.

(A moment. Then, in Hotel:)

JOSIE: *(On phone.)* I can't sing it without you. I don't remember the words.

(Beat.)

Well, start me off.

(She begins to sing haltingly, "Isn't It A Lovely Day" as her lover fills in the words.)

"The weather is frightening. The thunder and lightening, seem to be having their way — but as far as I'm concerned, it's a lovely —

(Losing the connection.)

Are you there? Are you there?

(Josie's phone goes dead.)

(In Shelter:)

VOLUNTEER: Is there a Hannah here?

GIRL: I'm Hannah.

VOLUNTEER: Got a message. *(He hands her a note.)*

GIRL: *(Reading out loud.)* "Dearest Hannah. Are you safe? I need to know. Are you safe? Tell me. Just let me hear that you are safe." *(Looking up.)* Is it from my father?

VOLUNTEER: *(Looking at the envelope.)* It's from your husband!

(EVERYONE laughs.)

I guess I made a mistake.

SEYMOUR: Maybe it's from her future husband.

GIRL: I'm never going to get married. Maybe I'll marry a girl.

RACHEL: That's cool. I mean, it's modern.

GIRL: Maybe I won't get married at all. I'll be too busy.

WINNIE: I can just see you all grown up. All busy and all grown up.

SEYMOUR: It'll work out. It'll work out just fine for her.

GIRL: I guess he was looking for a different Hannah.

SEYMOUR: Coffee's good. Coffee's what I needed.

WINNIE: *(To SEYMOUR.)* You made iced tea out there. On the porch. Iced tea or lemonade. You used to fight with your wife out there.

SEYMOUR: Sometimes we'd fight. It was nothing.

WINNIE: It was like the sound of trees. The sound that trees make. It was part of things. Your porch.

SEYMOUR: We start from scratch. It'll be a relief. A relief to just —

WINNIE: You know the funny thing — what was left was something I thought I lost. A key to — I don't even know what. And the words to a song I've been trying to remember for years.

(In Hotel, JOSIE *holds her phone and sings, even though the phone is dead.)*

JOSIE: "The turn in the weather, will keep us together, so I can honestly say, that as far as I'm concerned it's a lovely day. And everything's okay. Isn't it a lovely day to be caught in the rain. You were going on your way now you have to remain —"

(In Shelter:)

SEYMOUR: I got old. When did I get old? It just now happened. I'm old.

(The GIRL *holds up a sheet of paper.)*

GIRL: Here's my dog.

SEYMOUR: I don't see a dog.

GIRL: I wrote him. He's a written dog. He's a wordy dog. He's a dog of words.

SEYMOUR: Well. That's clever. You're a clever young lady.

GIRL: *(Reading from her paper.)* My dog is not in a commercial.

My dog is foolish for me.

My dog is just like your dog. Belonging.

This dog jumps for joy.

Dog jumps for reasons known only to him.

My dog knows who loves him. Dog knows everything you need to know.

WINNIE: From how you put it, there's definitely a dog in my mind.

RACHEL: You see them trying to get home. They'll do anything for you. They want to come back.

SEYMOUR: How did you think of that? Of what you said. How did you come up with that?

WINNIE: You were so good in that play. She was a writer, wasn't she? The young girl. She would have grown up to be a writer.

SEYMOUR: You know how when something happens to other people, when this or that happens. On the news. In the paper. And you read about it. Or you see them on television, trying to get a sentence out, trying to make words out of losing something that mattered so much they can't even remember how to breathe. And you'd do anything to take what happened off their hearts. But then you can't stand to know about it anymore.

WINNIE: *(A beat.)* You kids going to put on another play? Next time it should be a musical! Nothing terrible ever happens in a musical.

SEYMOUR: *(Coming back to himself.)* There's not too much mud in a musical.

RACHEL: I could paint the scenery.

WINNIE: *Pajama Game!* Or *Oklahoma!*

SEYMOUR: *(Starts to sing.)* "Oklahoma, where the wind comes —" what? Comes what?

VOLUNTEER: *(Speaks the words.)* "Sweepin' down the plain."

SEYMOUR: *(Sings.)* "Sweepin' down the plain."

RACHEL: "Where the wavin' wheat —"

RACHEL AND SEYMOUR: "Can sure smell sweet — "

WINNIE: And the — something something — duh duh duh duh duh.

SEYMOUR AND WINNIE: "O—klahoma, every night my honey lamb and I — Sit alone and talk and watch a — "

VOLUNTEER: "Hawk."

ALL: *(Everyone joins in as it builds to a rousing chorus.)* "And watch a hawk. Makin' lazy circles in the sky. We know we belong to the land. And the land we belong to is grand. And when we say — Yo! Aye yip Ayo Eyay! We're only sayin', you're doin' fine, Oklahoma. Oklahoma, okay!"

(They falter for a moment, until WINNIE brings everyone back to the song.)

"We know we belong to the land. And the land we belong to is grand. And when we say — Yo! Ay yip Ayo Eyay! we're only sayin', you're doin' fine, Oklahoma. Oklahoma — "

VOLUNTEER: "O - K — "

ALL: "L - A - H - O - M - A — OKLAHOMA!"

(The SINGING STOPS suddenly, as their reality sets it. After a moment, JOSIE continues singing from her HOTEL ROOM. Still, not able to make a phone connection, but making a larger one.)

JOSIE: *(Singing.)* "Let the rain pitter patter cause it really doesn't matter if the sky is blue. Long as I can be with you, it's a lovely day."

(Beat.)

I'm here. I'm here.

(LIGHTS FADE)

In The Screening Room

A private screening room in a Hollywood studio. The stage is set with three theatre seats Stage Left and one or two chairs on the Right, separated by a space that represents an aisle. We hear the TAPPING OF DANCING FEET *and Fred Astaire singing, "Isn't It A Lovely Day," as the movie* Top Hat *plays. A* LIGHT *comes from the projection booth behind the seats. A* DOOR *opens. In the shaft of light, the* EDITOR *walks in, confused. He's obviously wandered into the wrong place. He looks around, then at the movie screen. Begins to dance along with it. Then catches himself. And he leaves.*

Music continues. After a moment, MAGGIE, *a film studio executive, walks in. She also is taken with Astaire. And begins to dance. Suddenly the aging projectionist,* MEYER, *speaks to her from the booth.*

MEYER: Maggie.

MAGGIE: God, you scared me.

(MEYER *continues talking from the booth, and we never actually see him.*)

MEYER: Nice gams. You got grace.

MAGGIE: I have bunions. And respect for the man *(signifying Astaire)* who's got grace. Did we hear anything from Josie yet?

MEYER: She dropped off the last reel. Finished.

MAGGIE: Josie never finishes. There'll be changes.

(Notices tulips in a vase.)

Who brought the tulips?

MEYER: That young man works for you. The one with the college degree.

MAGGIE: They all have college degrees.

MEYER: The one who likes you.

MAGGIE: They all "like" me. They have to.

MEYER: The one you like.

MAGGIE: Ah. What are we doing here, Meyer?

MEYER: It's a place to be.

MAGGIE: *(With a light touch, but meaning it.)* Let's change the world.

MEYER: Sure. Why not.

MAGGIE: Don't shrug it off, my friend.

MEYER: People wandering in here, you should know.

MAGGIE: *(Looking at film.)* I love this part. I love how they just — that step!

(Door opens as BOBBY, *a creative development V.P and another V.P.,* DONALD, *walk in.* MAGGIE *shuts off the film and switches gears.)*

MAGGIE: So, this is what I know. They're looking for a female *Death of a Salesman.*

DONALD: I didn't hear this.

MAGGIE: I'm telling you this.

DONALD: I didn't know this.

MAGGIE: That's the mandate.

DONALD: I don't see how you can —

MAGGIE: A female Willy Loman. *Death of a Saleswoman.*

DONALD: That's what they want.

MAGGIE: That's what they're saying.

(A subtle conspiratorial nod.)

Bobby?

BOBBY: That's what they're saying.

MAGGIE: Any number of women out there. Meryl Streep. Any number of female Willys.

DONALD: Meryl Streep can't sell a movie.

BOBBY: Well, Julia Roberts, then.

DONALD: And, what, then the sons —

MAGGIE: Daughters.

DONALD: Daughters. Right. They'd be — of course.

MAGGIE: Clare Danes. Gwyneth Paltrow. Plenty of daughters.

BOBBY: Winona.

DONALD: You've got me thinking.

MAGGIE: Good. Good.

DONALD: I'm thinking.

MAGGIE: We'll need a writer, of course. To adapt Miller. Or Miller.

DONALD: Oh, you're thinking Miller.

BOBBY: Why not Miller?

DONALD: Sure. Why not. Except. Except, Miller's up there. Isn't he? Miller's a tad — what's he, sixty-something?

MAGGIE: Eighty-something.

DONALD: Get a couple of young guys. Big smiles. Good hair.

MAGGIE: They'd need the good hair, to re-write *Salesman*.

DONALD: I'm just remarking.

MAGGIE: No. You're bringing your observations to bear. I understand.

(Beat.)

She could be one gorgeous Willy.

DONALD: This is something to mull.

MAGGIE: This is the mandate.

DONALD: We could turn a corner. Our names on this?

MAGGIE: It's ours.

DONALD: I'm going to town on it. My heart's thumping. *Death of a Saleswoman.*

(MAGGIE starts to laugh. BOBBY breaks up with her. As it becomes clear she's putting DONALD on.)

DONALD: What? No. Jesus.

MAGGIE: Oh. Come on.

DONALD: Now, I'm excited about the project.

MAGGIE: It's not a project.

DONALD: We go to them with it. We get a buzz.

MAGGIE: One gorgeous Willy.

DONALD: Why not?

MAGGIE: A flaw like that — a flaw like that in a man — it's worthy. We have pity. A woman like that we'd despise. A woman starts off down. Finds her way out. A man falls, we feel this in our hearts. But, a woman's situation — a woman comes to strength, that's seen as who she's leaving behind, who she abandons. A woman comes on stage looking like Lee J. Cobb, Dustin Hoffman, we don't want to look. We don't want to see a woman brought to her knees. She can bring a man down. She can ruin someone. Or she can walk out, die of her own hand. We admire her maybe, but we don't feel this in our hearts.

(The Rear DOOR OPENS. *An eager young female Studio* TOUR GUIDE *appears with an* OLDER WOMAN.

We hear snatches of her spiel as she starts to enter.)

TOUR GUIDE: Excuse me. Sorry to interrupt —

DONALD: I keep telling you people. We're not a stop on the tour.

TOUR GUIDE: We have a very special visitor. I'd like you to meet the wife of the late playwright, Eugene Ionesco.

BOBBY: *(In awe.)* I did my master's thesis on *The Bald Soprano!*

*(*MADAME IONESCO *beams. She understands English but can't speak it well.)*

TOUR GUIDE: They came to Hollywood together on this same tour and it is their anniversary.

MAGGIE: *(Surprised and awed. Rising to greet her.)* I'm so — It's such a rare — I'm —

TOUR GUIDE: She doesn't really speak much English.

MAGGIE: Of course. I'm sorry. I —

*(*MADAME IONESCO *begins to speak in French. As the* TOUR GUIDE *translates.)*

TOUR GUIDE: She wants to tell you that Monsieur Ionesco loved the American movie. And — especially he adored Fred Astaire and Rita Hayworth.

MAGGIE: Yes. *Oui! Il et un grande* —

(She stops herself)

TOUR GUIDE: *(Continuing to translate, haltingly)* Also — Madame Ionesco loves the Annie Hall.

(Beat.)

You gave her husband such joy. Countless hours.

MAGGIE: Not so much *I*. I haven't.

PLAYWRIGHT'S WIFE: *Mes problemes s'evanouissent comme ca: Pfuit!*

TOUR GUIDE: My problems they go poof! He would say.

(A starkly quiet moment. Then, in English:)

PLAYWRIGHT'S WIFE: Enraptured.

(MADAME IONESCO and the TOUR GUIDE leave. MAGGIE is a bit shaken.)

BOBBY: Are you — you all right?

MAGGIE: No, I'm fine. I'm — fine.

(Pulling herself together,)

So, what do we have? What are we seeing?

DONALD: It's — I believe it's — it's the — you have it there in the—

BOBBY: It's the Sugarman.

MAGGIE: Sugarman. Is this the guy we're supposed to be impressed how mean he is?

BOBBY: That's a different guy.

MAGGIE: We're supposed to be impressed by his daring meanness.

BOBBY: People are like that.

MAGGIE: People are not so happy to be like that. They are not so pleased with themselves to be like that. Are they?

BOBBY: I don't know.

MAGGIE: Are they?

BOBBY: Well, this is not that guy.

DONALD: The Sugarman has promise.

BOBBY: He's got promise, Sugarman.

DONALD: Everyone's calling it the new —

MAGGIE: Everyone?

DONALD: Everyone in town. Everyone who's —

MAGGIE: Everyone.

DONALD: In town. Bowled over, I think is how they —

MAGGIE: Meyer, do you have your tea up there?

BOBBY: He's set. He's fine with the tea.

(As LIGHTS *in the room begin to dim.)*

MAGGIE: You know how someone will say — is always saying "the Jack Kennedys of the world" or the — the — the Eleanor Roosevelts or the Chekhovs, as if — as if — we're just overrun with them. Does this bother you? I am so bothered by that.

(She seems to settle, then abruptly:)

Who are we disappointing at this very minute. That's what I'm thinking about. What brings a person to her knees. That's the story. That's the only story.

(LIGHTS DIM in the room. Flicker from the screen and projection booth. Everyone watches.)

MAGGIE: *(Recalling Ionesco.)* My problems they go "Poof!"

(Then, after a moment, MAGGIE *picks up the phone and dials. Then speaks into it.)*

MAGGIE: It's me. I can't stop thinking about last night. When did you turn into a selfish man? I'm not glad to be saying this. You're pushing me. You're pushing me to something. I'm just sick about — where are you? Why do you go to that awful place? Everyone's always there and there is nothing distinguishable about it. We're all becoming a chain. Chain people that's what we are.

(Beat, almost to herself.)

Everything was possible and now it isn't.

(She hangs up. She turns her attention to the screen for an instant. Concentrating only on what she sees. Then picks up the phone to make another call.)

MAGGIE: Sweetie. You there? Pick up. No. Okay. Well, it's me. Mom. Just wanting to — to tell you things. Do you want to drive later? I'm going to have some time so we can take the car out because I think you need a little practice. We can drive and get sushi afterwards or pick up a pizza.

(She hangs up. She continues watching the movie for an instant. Then calls, "Okay Meyer," to end it.)

DONALD: Sugarman. He has promise, don't you think?

BOBBY: Should we — set up something? A lunch.

MAGGIE: A lunch.

BOBBY: With Sugarman.

MAGGIE: I don't want to have lunch with Sugarman. He doesn't want to have lunch with me.

(To booth.)

Meyer, did you think the Sugarman had promise?

(Beat.)

[72]

He heard me. He hears everything. He heard me. Meyer doesn't want to get involved.

DONALD: Fox is after him. They want to get into bed with him. They want to be in the Sugarman business.

BOBBY: Look, maybe if —

MAGGIE: Just what is this movie about? What does it mean?

DONALD: It doesn't necessarily mean —

MAGGIE: Don't you think —

DONALD: What?

MAGGIE: Don't you think that it has to —

DONALD: What?

MAGGIE: Mean something.

(Pause.)

Is it me or — aren't you sad?

BOBBY: Sugarman did this to you? Ten minutes of Sugarman did this?

MAGGIE: I just want this to be something I need to see. I just want this with all my heart.

DONALD: He's going to be big. He's on his way. He's going to be tremendous.

MAGGIE: And sad.

DONALD: I could take him to lunch. Just to keep it going.

MAGGIE: My friend Elaine. Said this brilliant thing in the kitchen the other day. Casually in the kitchen a person spoke in her true voice. No one is taking her to lunch but she is brilliant in the kitchen. She is a fucking genius. And beautiful. But like most women she doesn't know it. No one particularly wants to be in the Elaine business. Naturally, she's on antidepressants. Being the only person in the 21st century who hasn't written a movie.

DONALD: So, is that a pass?

MAGGIE: I mean, what happens in here is not the test.

BOBBY: What happens in here.

DONALD: In this room?

MAGGIE: In here. What happens in this place. It's not the test.

DONALD: The test.

MAGGIE: The test of a person. How you're called upon.

(Beat.)

How you conduct yourself.

BOBBY: Your character, you're saying. Maybe it takes your whole life to know what that is.

MAGGIE: It can happen in a minute. It usually happens in a minute.

BOBBY: Maybe you don't realize.

MAGGIE: That it's happened.

BOBBY: That it's happened. Right. Maybe you don't know that in a minute.

DONALD: What the hell. What the hell.

MAGGIE: I think you know it. I think you just don't know what to call it. What it means to the rest of your life. In relation to everything else.

DONALD: We've got a meeting at the end of the day. We've got to make a decision here. We've got to make something happen.

MAGGIE: Your child. Say your child asks a hard question. You want to protect him. But he's counting on you to tell him what he needs to know. Or your friend's husband says he's thinking about sleeping with someone else. What do you do? I mean how do you live with what you know? This isn't the place for the test.

BOBBY: Aren't we trying to bring something to light? Something good.

MAGGIE: You're in the market, Bobby. It's the marketplace.

(*The* DOOR OPENS. *The* TOUR GUIDE *enters with* TWO PEO-PLE.)

DONALD: (*About to lose it.*) What?

TOUR GUIDE: I want to introduce Sarah Cabot Jones who won the coveted MacArthur "Genius" Prize for her series of poems, "Dead Poets at the Movies."

MAGGIE: I know your book! It's wonderful. *Auden On The Aisle.* It was so —

DONALD: Auden. Isn't he quoted in the next Spielberg?

POET: Auden's mother used to take him to the movies in the afternoons. They'd see a double feature. They were both mad for Cary Grant. It was their church.

BOBBY: I had such a crush on him.

POET: For me, it's the kiss. The movie kiss. Larger than the length of our days. A kiss to eclipse our miseries. The rapture!

TOUR GUIDE: And I'd also like you to meet Mr. Joe Cerullo, a firefighter who pulled three children to safety and went back into a burning building to find their dog.

FIREMAN: This is a terrific thrill for me.

MAGGIE: (*Moved by him.*) No, it's *our* thrill. It's our privilege.

FIREMAN: My father threw fists. We'd run away. Sneak into the pictures. Talk up at the screen, ya know, say the words with them. See it over and over again. Had the words by heart.

(Beat, as he looks around.)

Man! All my heroes!

(They leave. Maggie is visibly affected. Bobby observing her.)

BOBBY: I think if we — if we just went ahead and looked at the next one. Maggie?

(The door opens. The TOUR GUIDE *brings another visitor, a* YOUNG GIRL.*)*

TOUR GUIDE: I'd like you to meet Anya Divac. Anya's written a diary of her days in the war-torn former Yugoslavia.

MAGGIE: It's an honor!

YOUNG GIRL: *(Haltingly.)* I — do not know the correct way to be, to grow to be a woman. But in the movies — I see others with my anxieties.

(Beat.)

Things are said. Things are said here, that I, too, think about but I'm not bold enough to —

(Beat.)

Our worries — they go into hiding.

(They leave. Maggie is moved and disturbed by the girl's visit.)

MAGGIE: This is not what I really am. You know that. This is not something someone really is. If you don't get out of this, you'll be my successor to the position of not being what you are. But you can only say that for so long. Because, then you are exactly this. You are not what you were or thought you were. You are this.

DONALD: *(The height of impatience.)* Can we please —

Can we please —

BOBBY: Yeah. All right. Okay.

(To the Booth.)

Meyer, can we have the Josie Friedlander.

(To Maggie.)

There aren't any credit sequences yet. She's changing the title. I think we're going to see the scene where —

MAGGIE: No. Don't say. Let's just —

Lights dim on the room, as LIGHT *from the projection booth streams in. Meyer and Maggie watch the screen, as they give a verbal narrative of the film. This should come across with rapture, surprise, and, for Maggie, personal resonance.*

MEYER: She. Walks into the room. He doesn't see her there. She's a stranger to him in this place. Her voice. Something like his wife.

MAGGIE: He knows her.

MEYER: You never knew me.

MAGGIE: It's not what she says. It's what he says to himself. It is exactly what she wants to say.

MEYER: She walks in again. Cut to: Cut to: She walks into the room again. Until finally. It's you. They hold a gaze. Good to see you here.

MAGGIE: Has he spoken? I had to come. I needed to come.

Good you're here.

She can't stay. I can't stay.

Here? Now?

With you.

MEYER: The light from the window plays on them. Filled with dust. Moments pass. All that moves is the air.

I brought you a shirt.

Is what he hears her say.

MAGGIE: She means, I want to take care of you. But I have to go. What's over belongs to him now. What's over is his. Like all the lost people who find their way to him. She's leaving. She's joining the world. She's not his. You were never mine, she says.

MEYER: Stop. Wait. Don't. Now he remembers her. The one next to him. Every day. She says interesting things. She is often beautiful. She arouses him.

I have to go.

MAGGIE: Because a woman will know when it's time. But, the going is not in her bones.

It's terrible. Forgive me.

MEYER: He is like so many other men now. She's gone.

A window at the corner of the office. He does not walk over to it where he could see her again. He walks to his desk. He sits. He reviews every one else's history. He opens the mail.

MAGGIE: She knows this from the street. Where we see her walking. She knows what he is doing from a history of knowing what he does. Except he is not at his desk. The mail is tossed to the floor. He's standing at the window.

MEYER: "Everyone wants to know how it will turn out," she says later. In the first line. Of the book she's writing. It will change many times. The first line. And the last.

(The lights are restored to normal in the room. There is that briefly odd sensory moment of moving suddenly from the created world to the real one. It overtakes Maggie.)

MAGGIE: If I could just sit here a minute.

DONALD: So, you — ?

MAGGIE: I'd just like to sit here a minute.

DONALD: You're saying —

MAGGIE: I just need to —

DONALD: Then you liked it.

MAGGIE: What does that mean? I like a nice glass of Merlot. I like — oh god. Did *you* like it?

DONALD: I was just responding to your response. I was trying to ascertain what you thought of it.

MAGGIE: Well, but, what did you think of it?

DONALD: What did I think?

MAGGIE: What did you think?

DONALD: What did I think.

MAGGIE: Be brave, Donald.

DONALD: I'm just — no, I mean. It's all there. It's — if you liked it —

MAGGIE: So, then, what are you telling me that you only liked it?

DONALD: This is your pick, then?

MAGGIE: Don't you know what we've seen here? Doesn't this mean something to you?

BOBBY: Now, listen. Now, Maggie. Now, just a minute. To be fair.

MAGGIE: *(Upset.)* Can't anyone ever say what a thing is? Just what a thing is to them. Is it too much to ask of people that they just tell you what a thing is?

(She gets up and leaves the room.)

DONALD: Well. Well, that was — what? What do you — make of it?

BOBBY: She's going through something.

DONALD: Oh. Didn't know.

BOBBY: What it was was that was passion.

DONALD: Well, I've never seen it before.

(Long pause.)

I'm concerned now. I feel, somehow, really, I feel in jeopardy. Somehow.

BOBBY: It'll work out.

DONALD: What? What will? My career. Our jobs. My children. Their children?

BOBBY: She'll be back and the future of your children will be insured. Jesus. With the children. Some of us, actually want —

DONALD: All right. I know. That was —

BOBBY: I want children. I very much want —

DONALD: You and your — partner.

BOBBY: We're talking about it.

DONALD: You and your partner?

BOBBY: We're talking about it.

DONALD: That's —

BOBBY: People are doing it.

DONALD: No, I know. That's —

BOBBY: I think children —

DONALD: He feels this way?

BOBBY: Children are the answer. Somehow.

DONALD: And your partner, he feels —

(Beat.)

Don't you worry that —

BOBBY: Here it comes. Here it comes.

DONALD: I'm just — look—

BOBBY: You're worried that —

DONALD: All right.

BOBBY: You're worried a child needs —

DONALD: A child needs — yes.

BOBBY: A mother and —

DONALD: A mother and a father.

BOBBY: A child needs a friend and a dog. A child needs an uncle and a toy and a teacher and something to eat and a book and a good example.

DONALD: Look. Now, look.

(MAGGIE returns. A new energy.)

MAGGIE: I want you to come to my house! I want to cook for you. I want you to come. This week-end. With your — your — with anyone who matters.

BOBBY: Really. It's not necessary. Really.

MAGGIE: I want you to come. You'll come and —

DONALD: That's all right.

MAGGIE: We'll talk about things.

BOBBY: Really, though.

MAGGIE: I mean it. You'll come this week-end. And we'll talk. We'll really talk.

(*Beat.*)

Where were we? I lost my place.

BOBBY: You were standing up for something.

DONALD: I honestly think you should give Sugarman a shot.

MAGGIE: All right, bring him. To my house. Sunday. I'll ask Elaine. Is he single, Sugarman?

DONALD: I'll put a call in to his agent.

(DONALD *leaves.*)

BOBBY: Anything you need before I leave?

MAGGIE: Where do you go after work? What do you do?

BOBBY: I'm — I usually — tonight, my friend, she's a singer. We're going to hear her sing.

MAGGIE: That's my idea of a night.

BOBBY: I didn't know.

MAGGIE: Well, how could you?

BOBBY: Would you — I mean, do you want to — you could meet us there.

MAGGIE: Oh, no. No. I was just — well, anyway. Thanks.

(BOBBY stands for a moment, unsure.)

MAGGIE: Go. Really.

BOBBY: Josie's film.

(Beat)

I thought it was really good.

MAGGIE: *(Moved)* The tulips, They're so encouraging.

(He's gone. The DOOR OPENS. The EDITOR walks in.)

EDITOR: Hannah?

MAGGIE: *(Caught off guard.)* Darling?

(Both realize they are not who they thought they were.)

EDITOR: Excuse me. I thought —

MAGGIE: I'm sorry.

EDITOR: I think I might be lost.

MAGGIE: Welcome to the place for that.

EDITOR: I was on a — tour and I wandered off. I walked on to a movie set. It was a newspaper office. It was a pretty damn nice newspaper office. Anyhow, it gets you to question the real thing. After that everything else is a disappointment. Coming home to an actual living room, an actual kiss.

MAGGIE: You called me *Hannah*.

EDITOR: You said *darling*.

MAGGIE: A slip.

EDITOR: *(Feeling a connection.)* The same for me.

MAGGIE: You were looking for her?

EDITOR: There's always someone you're looking for. You're always looking.

MAGGIE: I think more often I'm looking for reasons.

EDITOR: What do you do here?

MAGGIE: Decide things. I look at other people's work. And decide about it. I've made mistakes.

EDITOR: Yes.

MAGGIE: I haven't always been —

EDITOR: I know that situation.

MAGGIE: I think my marriage is over.

EDITOR: I'm sorry.

(Beat.)

Though, not necessarily. This is America.

MAGGIE: Okay. Look, I don't want to tell you things.

EDITOR: People tell me things. That's what happens.

MAGGIE: What did you mean, about America?

EDITOR: Waste. Revision. Hope.

MAGGIE: You didn't come with an idea for a screenplay, did you?

EDITOR: I need my ideas too much. When I have them. To give them away.

(Beat.)

Maybe you've heard of this movie —*What Harry Knows?*

MAGGIE: Josie Friedlander's film! I just saw a rough cut. I almost came to blows over it.

(Beat.)

The title's changing.

EDITOR: Harry's gone?

MAGGIE: Well, he didn't seem like a Harry, even in the book.

EDITOR: At the end of things, you lose your name. You aren't anyone.

MAGGIE: You're someone else.

EDITOR: It's just — you don't know who yet.

MAGGIE: *(Making the connection now between him and Hannah.)* There's love in it. That hasn't changed. From the book. Just no hope it'll go on being what you need it to be.

EDITOR: If you could, what would you say? To make it work.

MAGGIE: I'd say, there's nothing left to say. To him.

EDITOR: Maybe you have to say it to someone else.

MAGGIE: What would you say? Next time.

EDITOR: I'd say everything.

MAGGIE: *(After a moment.)* Do you want to screen it? The movie. Would you like to see it.

EDITOR: *(Giving up something.)* I thought I did.

(A moment.)

MAGGIE: Look, why don't we get out of here and go somewhere actual?

(The door opens and a breathless YOUNG MAN/SUGARMAN walks in. MAGGIE doesn't know him. Thinks he's one more hapless tourist.)

MAGGIE: You ditched the tour. You wandered off. Now you're lost. Plenty of room.

SUGARMAN: I'm here to apologize.

MAGGIE: Perfect. Who are you?

SUGARMAN: Please, just let me get this out of the way. It was — what — it was arrogance or — I don't know. It was misguided, for sure. See, you're pushing 25, you're encouraged anyone takes the time. Someone, maybe the waitress in a coffee shop gives you her pencil when you lost yours somewhere. Signs like that. Or a teacher tells you what you wrote was pretty good. Even original. And the thing is, you're allowed. Everyone has this permission to make something out of nothing. Well, to try, anyhow. I just didn't come up to it. I'm so sorry.

(To the air.)

Sorry, Mom.

MAGGIE: Look, your mother's probably proud of you. She's glad for your existence. Your mother is, I feel I can speak reassuringly here, completely concerned for your safety and well-being and all the rest — doesn't matter.

(The DOOR opens and the TOUR GUIDE pops in. At the sight of the EDITOR, she is almost ecstatic in her relief.)

TOUR GUIDE: Oh, Mr. Holiday. I'm so glad to see you. I thought we lost you! Well, here you are!

(To Maggie.)

I'm sorry. This is Ben Holiday, the Pulitzer Prize-winning journalist.

(Recognizing Sugarman.)

And Mr. Sugarman, you're supposed to be in a meeting. They're looking for you in the main office.

MAGGIE: You're Sugarman!

EDITOR: You're the one. Who wrote me that letter.

MAGGIE: Are you aware everyone wants to take you to lunch?

SUGARMAN: That's over. I'm stopping that.

MAGGIE: I like you, then.

TOUR GUIDE: We have a lot of other things left to see.

MAGGIE: *(Waving her off.)* They've seen it. They know what it is. We're fine here.

(The TOUR GUIDE *leaves.)*

EDITOR: You're Sugarman. You're the young man who wants to apologize to his mother.

SUGARMAN: The work. I want it back. I'm taking it back.

MAGGIE: You're going around recalling your work.

SUGARMAN: It's not mine. I mean, it's not what I'd say. If I had anything to say.

EDITOR: You wrote in to my column. You thought you made a mistake going into the film business. You wanted to make it up to your mother, somehow.

SUGARMAN: I let her down. People are going to let people down, aren't they? They're going to sink to the bottom. They aren't always going to be redeemable. Maybe that's what I should have said.

(Beat.)

Or a good thing happens. You catch something good in someone. The goodness. I could have written that.

MAGGIE: You know, Sugarman, I wasn't completely looking. Your film, I didn't really see it. I was caught up in a problem. I wasn't looking.

SUGARMAN: If it was anything to look at you'd have been looking. It's just this ugly feeling to put your name on something less than what you wanted it to be. I'm seeing how that stinks up the whole endeavor. There's harm in that.

MAGGIE: Oh, god. Thank you for this boy. You're right. You're so young to be seeing it.

EDITOR: Well, it only matters when you're young. And when you realize you're not young. That's when everything matters.

SUGARMAN: What if — there's nothing. What if — jesus, there's nothing.

EDITOR: That's always the —

MAGGIE: Yes.

SUGARMAN: That's why I'm —

EDITOR: That's always the —

MAGGIE: Yes.

SUGARMAN: Why I don't know if I —

EDITOR: *(Finishing his thought.)* Can.

   (Beat.)

That's always the feeling. The feeling before.

SUGARMAN: I thought there was something.

EDITOR: We're stranded. We're lonely on the planet. So, if there's anything, Sugarman, you're obligated.

SUGARMAN: But, do you ever feel guilty? I mean, about where it comes from. Whose sorrows and failures it's built on.

(Beat.)

Do you love them, the people you write about?

EDITOR: I don't know. They're just mine.

(Beat.)

Your letter. It was lovely. You didn't hide anywhere. And this makes me think — this movie of yours you're taking back — maybe you wrote the wrong day.

(He's got their attention. As his idea grows.)

You wrote someone else's day. Well, someone else's version of a day. It wasn't yours.

(Beat.)

There's a day. Everyone's got this. A day that's yours. A day with your story in it. This is the day you have to write about. I mean, to see what's yours is a magnificent thing. And the hardest thing. But if you don't tell it, it's gone. No one else can bring it to light.

SUGARMAN: What if I go there — to that day or whatever and I don't see it? Or I don't know what it is. What it is I'm supposed to —

MAGGIE: Sugarman, there's a poet and a fireman and god knows the rest of us, and everyone's waiting for something to give them relief. This is what you can do.

SUGARMAN: What you saw. It's not —

MAGGIE: It's what I didn't see. It's the one you're going to write.

EDITOR: You don't know. You don't know what it is yet. The important thing is you go there.

SUGARMAN: *(After a breath.)* All right. All right.

(Slowly assuming authority and excitement as each piece of what he's about to create occurs to him)

I'll need a porch.

(Beat.)

I'll need a porch and a mother.

MAGGIE: I'll be your mother.

(The doors to the screening room open and we have a porch. They go toward it and ultimately sit down on the porch steps.)

EDITOR: What do you want me to do?

SUGARMAN: You're watching. You're watching from another place. You're my grandfather and you're watching. I like to think that, anyway.

EDITOR: I'm not here, then.

SUGARMAN: You're kind of here and not here.

EDITOR: But I'm watching.

SUGARMAN: I get the feeling of that. And you're not alone. There are other people with you. You're all watching. And my mother has something for me.

(Making the transformation, becoming his "mother," Maggie picks up something from step.)

MAGGIE: *(Using the Jewish word for grandfather.)* Zada's camera from the war.

(SUGARMAN continues to narrate, but he will soon drop this and enter the scene with his mother.)

SUGARMAN: It's a small moment. On a porch. Just before the stars come out.

MAGGIE: Sweetie! The stars!

SUGARMAN: One night before the stars come out. Before a solution is found. During the ordeal of people we can't see. Even though they're never far from us. It's personal — and it's not.

MAGGIE: It's a perfect night.

SUGARMAN: It's warm and perfect and it makes you want things to last.

MAGGIE: You said this thing one time. When you were little. You were crying desperately. Something I did or didn't do. Or wouldn't let you do, I guess. Well, you were unhappy and you said, "I wish there were two of you so I could punch the other Mommy in the face."

SUGARMAN: *(Fully entering the scene with her.)* I said that? Cool.

MAGGIE: It was kind of brilliant.

(Beat.)

This thing used to happen where — we'd be doing something, and all of a sudden I'd have this vision. Like when I was teaching you to drive and being such a nervous pain in the ass — well, anyhow, this thing would happen where I'd get this flash — of you, older. Of you at twenty or twenty-five. I'd get this sudden vision of what it would be like to put myself in your hands.

(Beat.)

And here we are.

SUGARMAN: I can't think how it would be to be — I mean — without your parents. I'd always want to tell you things.

MAGGIE: I'd always want you to.

EDITOR: Do I get to talk? You know, this might be a good place for a story from your grandfather.

SUGARMAN: He loved telling that story about the country club. Where I yell out to him. He's playing the 9th hole —

EDITOR: I'm playing the 9th hole and you're up on the hill with your mother at the pool. You're 7 . You're 7, jumping around. You see me in the distance. And you call out, "Zada!" "Zada!" Top of your lungs. Over the hush. In a place that wouldn't take Jews for so many years. "Zada!"

You're a boy who kisses his father and his Zada at the country club, on the street, wherever. You're a man, it's the same. Still, a kiss for us. Always a kiss for us.

(A Yiddish endearment:)

Taibeleh.

SUGARMAN: *(Something starting to gel.)* I can't make up my mind. exactly. What to do. I mean, the thing worth doing.

MAGGIE: I hope I'll always know everything you do. Even when I'm not here. Even after. I hope, even from such a great distance, it'll be something I can know. I think if you say it in your true voice, I'll know it. And so will everyone else.

SUGARMAN: *(An idea emerging.)* What do you think of this? I mean, it's just — you know, I don't know what it is yet — just — well —

(With growing excitement as the idea unfolds.)

There are these — people. There are these people. And you wonder what keeps them from sleep. Or how they missed their chances. And what they have to do with you.

(The rest of the cast begins to join the EDITOR *where he's standing, as they watch, assembled in positions or attire that we recognize from earlier. They are, in effect, Sugarman's fictional characters about to be born, as well as observers, citizens who will appreciate, or not, what he has to say, who will judge his work authentic or not. Our collective past and his personal future. And in the telling — in the way he approaches this emerging story — with wonder and engagement, we see why Sugarman has promise.)*

SUGARMAN: There are these people. Just having their conversations. Just having their conversations and their arguments. Their ideas about things. And these people live in the same city. They know the same streets. Only they don't know what it means that they know the same streets. Until something terrible happens. Not to someone else this time. To them.

Everything's lost. Or it seems that way.

(It starts to rain.)

There's rain. There's so much raining down on them.

(A DOG *comes in.)*

And a dog! There's rain and a dog. Everything's lost. And then something — maybe a dog finds its way home.

(Beat.)

And there's a girl!

(The YOUNG GIRL *steps forward.)*

This young girl. And she's taking it all in. She's writing it down. She's going to tell us how to live. Everything's lost and then a girl comes. A young girl with a funny remark. You know how kids will just have a funny remark. Everything's serious and then they'll say something you never thought of in your whole life the way they put it, and it makes you forget everything you were thinking about before that one moment.

(Beat, building)

There are all these people. And something terrible happens. But you know them now. They're yours. The woman who comes late to everything. And the man who's life might have been different if he asked a girl out.

(Beat)

There are all these people. And a dog finds its way back. And a young girl comes - a nice kid with a funny remark. And she makes everyone forget. And remember.

(Beat)

Then — out of the blue — just for no reason, the kid and the man and all these people, I don't know why, they all of a sudden sing!

(A long beat, then he emerges from his thoughts to address MAGGIE *and* EDITOR.*)*

It's only an idea.

EDITOR: That's only everything.

MAGGIE: What do they sing? Never mind. You don't have to know. You don't have to know that yet.

SUGARMAN: What do you think?

MAGGIE: *(Letting it fill her full with possibility.)* I like it.

SUGARMAN: So, you think I should –

MAGGIE: Tell us. Say it. Say what a thing is. What things could be. Don't spare us.

EDITOR: Be something we don't have yet.

SUGARMAN: Then, I should just –

MAGGIE: *(After a long beat.)* Continue.

(Lights fade.)

END OF PLAY

About the Author

Susan Miller, winner of the 2004 Pinter Review Prize for Drama and the Susan Smith Blackburn Prize, is the recipient of two OBIE awards and a Guggenheim Fellowship in playwriting. She is well known for her critically acclaimed one-woman play, *My Left Breast*, which premiered in Actor's Theatre of Louisville's Humana Festival, directed by Nela Wagman. The play has been performed by Miller and others in theatres across the United States, Canada, and Europe. It is published in *O Solo Homo* by Grove Press; and *Plays from the Humana Festival* by Smith and Kraus.

Miller won her first OBIE for *Nasty Rumors and Final Remarks*, produced in New York by Joseph Papp at the Public Theatre, as were her plays, *For Dear Life* and *Flux*, also produced by Second Stage. Her plays *Cross Country* and *Confessions of a Female Disorder* were staged by the Mark Taper Forum. Miller's other work includes *Arts and Leisure*; *It's Our Town, Too*, published in *Best American Short Plays* (Applause); and *The Grand Design*, a finalist for Actor's Theatre of Louisville's Heideman Prize, published in *Take Ten II* (Vintage). *The Grand Design* was performed by Lily Tomlin and Eric Stoltz in a benefit for Cure Autism Now, directed by Robert Egan, and was done by Marsha Mason and Scott Cohen for Brave New World. Miller's work has also been produced by Naked Angels, Trinity Repertory Co., The Walnut Street Theatre, and The Eugene O'Neill Playwrights Conference, among others.

Miller has received fellowships from the NEA, as well as a Rockefeller Grant and a residency at Yaddo and was awarded the Publishing Triangle's Lifetime Achievement Award in playwriting. She served for three years as the director of the Legacy Project, a writing workshop for people with life-threatening illness, held at the Public Theatre under a grant from the Lila Wallace Fund. She has taught in the Dramatic Writing Program at NYU; the Writer's Voice at the Westside Y; Rutgers; Penn State; and UCLA. Miller is an active member of the Dramatists Guild.

Her film and television work includes original feature screenplays for Disney, Warner Bros., Universal, Caravan, and Fox 2000, as well as the independent film, *Lady Beware*, starring Diane Lane. She has written for ABC's *thirtysomething*; CBS's *Trials of Rosie O'Neill*; NBC's *L.A. Law*, and FOX's *Urban Anxiety*, (Producer/Head Writer). Miller was a Consulting Producer on the first season of the breakthrough SHOWTIME series, *The L Word*.

About the Artist

Charlotte Salomon, whose painting appears on the dust jacket, was born in Berlin in 1917 and raised in a cultured German-Jewish environment. In 1939 amidst escalating Nazi atrocities, she followed her grandparents to the South of France. There her artistic work flourished, as she portrayed characters based on family and friends in simple texts and haunting paintings to form a unique verbal-visual lyrical drama she entitled *Life? or Theatre?*

In September 1943, just months after her marriage to Alexander Nagler, both were arrested in France by the Gestapo and transported to Auschwitz, where they were killed. Before she was deported, Salomon presented her gouaches to a family friend with the instruction: "Take good care of them. They are my whole Life."

Today the Jewish Historical Museum in Amsterdam preserves Salomon's masterpiece, including more than a thousand individual works. The Royal Academy of Arts in London selected four hundred pieces for a major exhibit in 1998 that toured to Toronto, Boston, and New York. Since that time, Salomon has become more widely known, and her reputation continues to grow.

About the Book

A Map of Doubt and Rescue is set in Adobe Garamond Pro types based on the sixteenth century roman types of Claude Garamond and the complementary italic types of Robert Granjon. They were adapted for digital composition by Robert Slimbach in consultation with colleagues including type historian and designer Steven Harvard, letterform expert John Lane, and Adobe's Fred Brady. Slimbach and Brady have written that Garamond's "roman types are arguably the best conceived typefaces ever designed, displaying a superb balance of elegance and practicality." The title of the book on the dust jacket and title page is set in Dyrynk Latinka, a font originally designed in 1929 by Karel Dyrynk, director of the government printing works and an important figure in the Czech book arts, adapted for digital release by the P22 foundry. The book was designed and typeset by Richard Mathews at the University of Tampa Press with a dust jacket in collaboration with Ana Montalvo. It has been printed on acid-free Glatfelter Natures Natural recycled text papers and bound in Savannah cloth by Thomson-Shore of Dexter, Michigan.